POPULAR GOSPEL SONGS

ISBN 978-1-4234-8933-7

HAL•LEONARD®
CORPORATION
7777 W. BLUEMOUND RD. P.O. BOX 13819 MILWAUKEE, WI 53213

Visit Hal Leonard Online at
www.halleonard.com

ANGEL BAND

Words and Music by
RALPH STANLEY

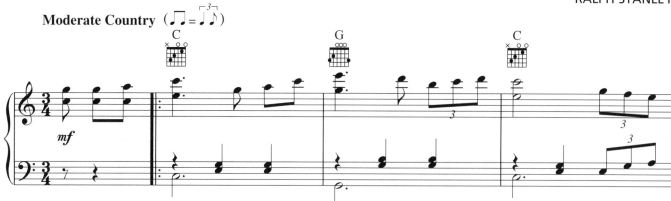

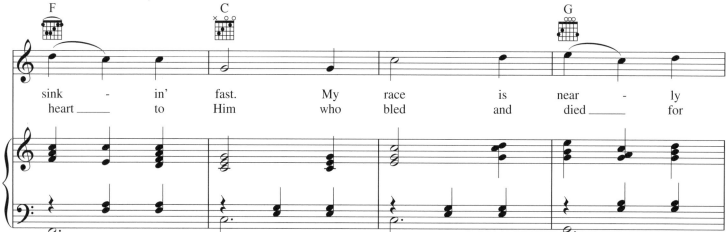

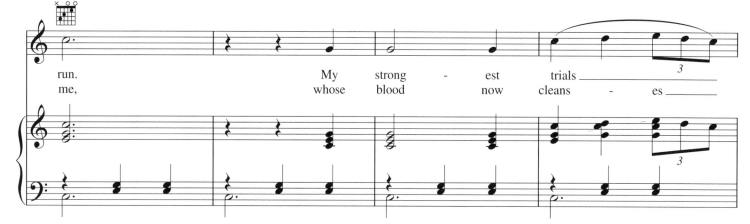

3

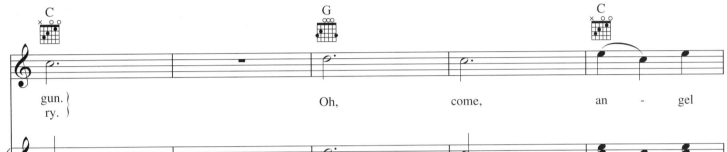

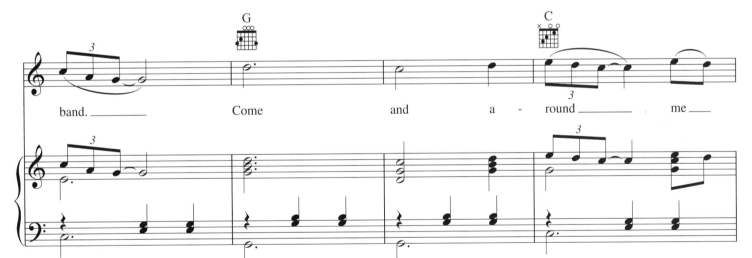

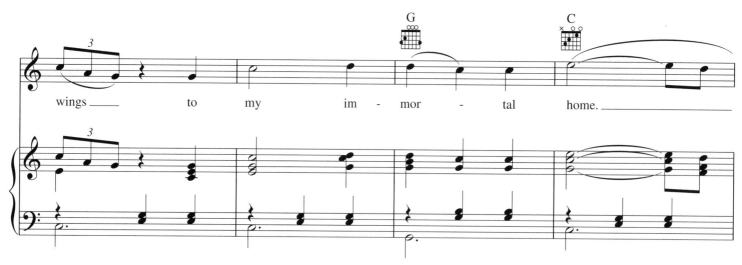

wings _____ to my im - mor - tal home. _____

_____ Oh, bear me a - way on your snow - white

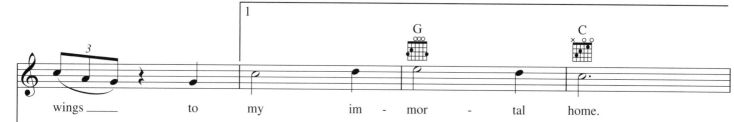

1

wings _____ to my im - mor - tal home.

2

my im - mor - tal home.

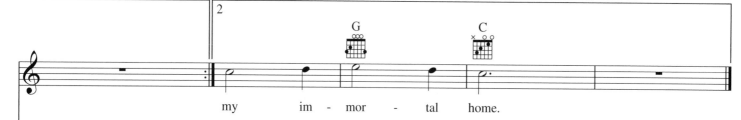

CRYING IN THE CHAPEL

Words and Music by
ARTIE GLENN

Slowly, with expression

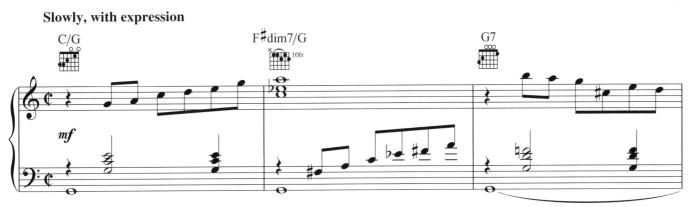

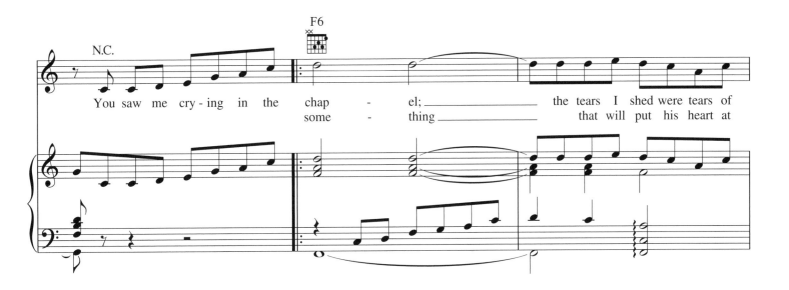

You saw me cry-ing in the chap-el; _____ the tears I shed were tears of
some-thing _____ that will put his heart at

joy. _____
ease. _____

I know the mean-ing of con-tent - ment, _____
There is on-ly one true an - swer: _____

BEAUTIFUL CITY
from GODSPELL

Music and Lyrics by
STEPHEN SCHWARTZ

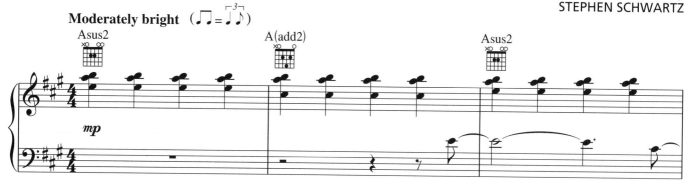

Out of the ruins and rub - ble,
We may not reach the end - ing,

out of the smoke, ___
but we can start ___
out of our night ___
slow - ly but tru -

___ of strug - gle, can we see ___ a ray of hope? ___
- ly mend - ing, brick by brick, ___ heart by heart. ___

One
Now,

pale thin ray, ___
may - be now, ___

reach - ing for the day. ___
we start learn - ing how. ___

We can build _____ a beau - ti - ful cit - y,

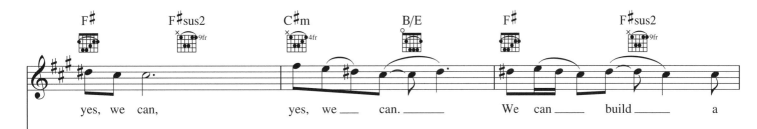

yes, we can, yes, we ___ can. _____ We can ___ build _____ a

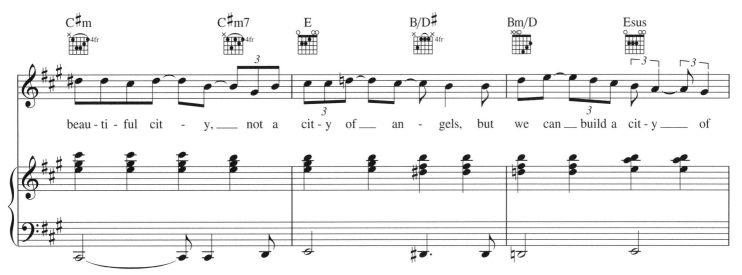

beau - ti - ful cit - y, ___ not a cit - y of ___ an - gels, but we can build a cit - y ___ of

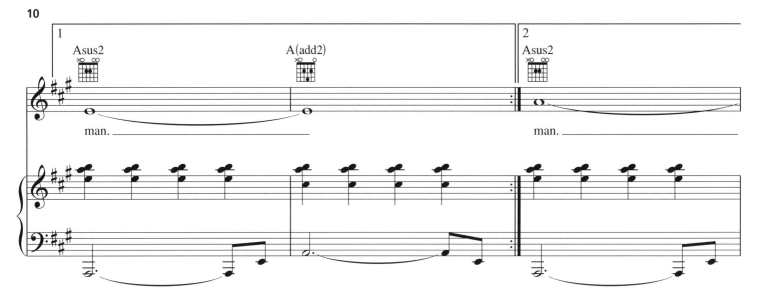

man. _____ man. _____

When your trust _____ is all but shat - tered, when your faith _____

_____ is all but killed, ___ you can give _____ up, bit - ter and bat -

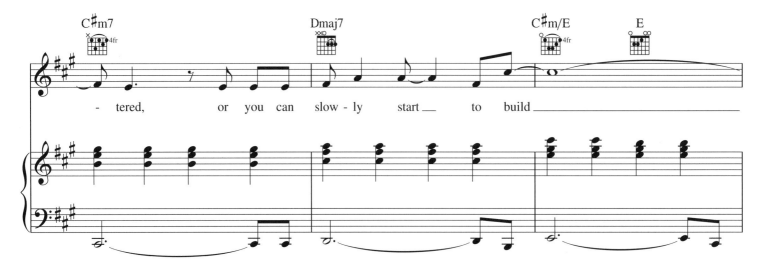

- tered, or you can slow - ly start ___ to build _____

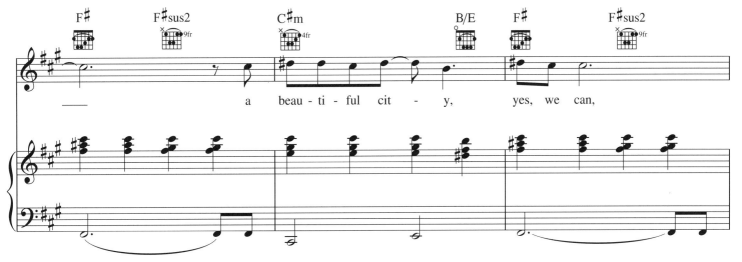

a beau - ti - ful cit - y, yes, we can,

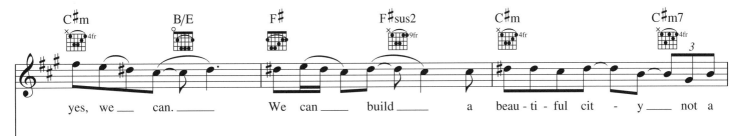

yes, we ___ can. ___ We can ___ build ___ a beau - ti - ful cit - y ___ not a

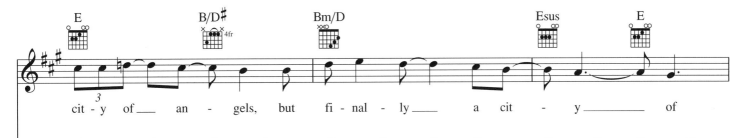

cit - y of ___ an - gels, but fi - nal - ly ___ a cit - y ___ of

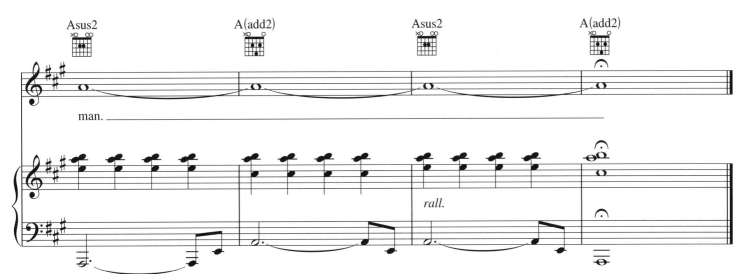

man. _____

rall.

DADDY SANG BASS

Words and Music by
CARL PERKINS

Moderately fast

I re - mem-ber when I was a lad, times were hard and things were bad. But there's a sil - ver lin - ing be - hind ev - 'ry cloud. _____ Just poor peo-ple, that's all we were, try-in' to make a liv-in' out of black land

dirt. We'd get to- geth- er in a fam- 'ly cir- cle, sing- in' loud. _____

_____ Dad- dy sang bass, Ma- ma sang ten- or. Me and lit- tle broth- er would join right

in there. Sing- in' seems to help a trou- bled soul. _____

_____ One of these days and it won't be long, I'll re - join them in a

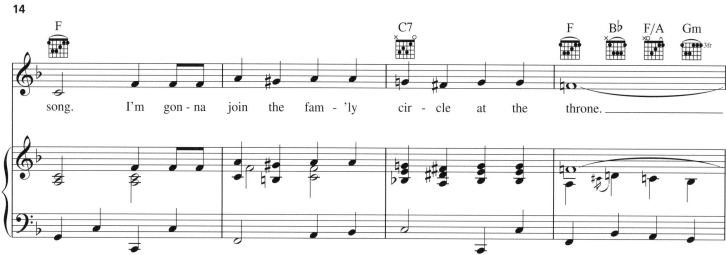

song. I'm gon-na join the fam-'ly cir-cle at the throne.

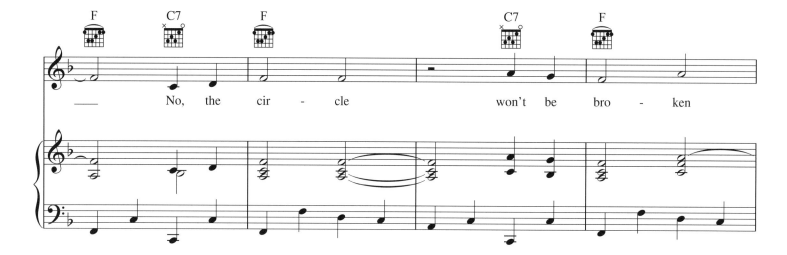

No, the cir - cle won't be bro - ken

by and by, Lord, by and by.

D.S. and Fade

Dad-dy-'ll sing bass, Ma-ma-'ll sing ten - or. Me and lit - tle broth-er will join right

DAY BY DAY
from the Musical GODSPELL

Music by STEPHEN SCHWARTZ
Lyrics by RICHARD OF CHICHESTER (1197-1253)

Easy Waltz feel

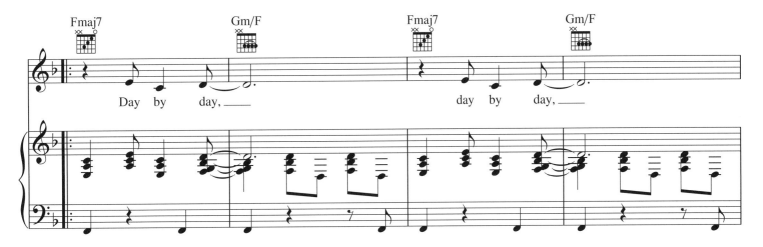

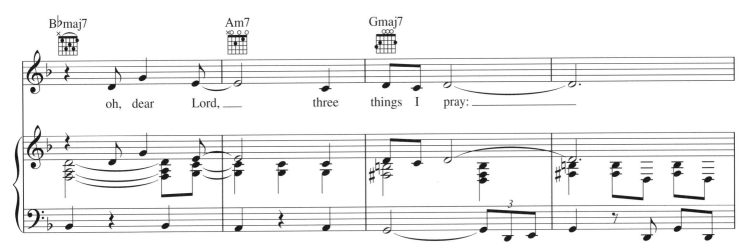

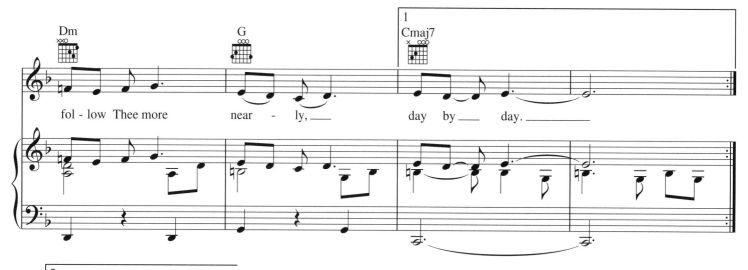

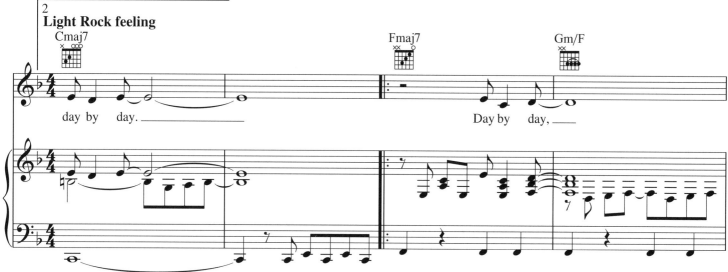

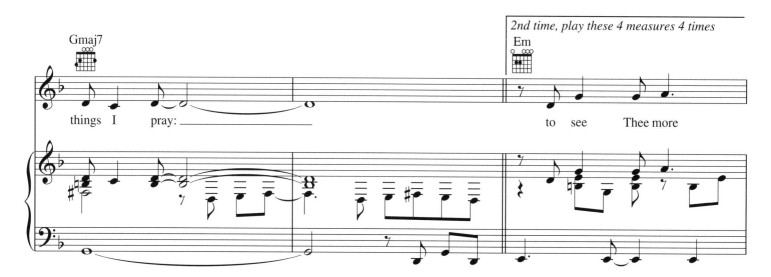

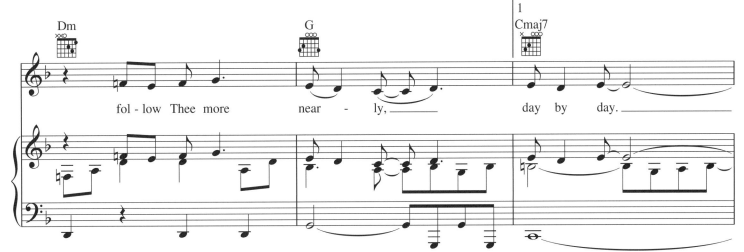

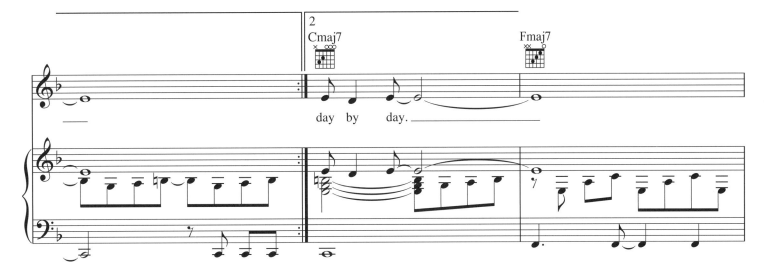

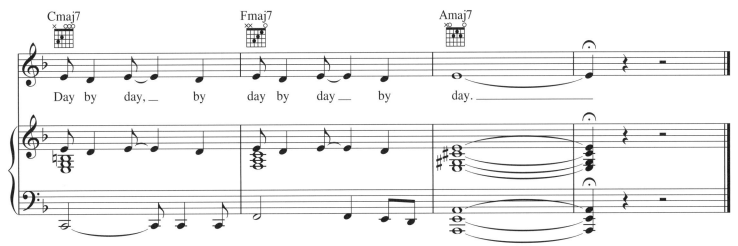

EVERYTHING IS BEAUTIFUL

Words and Music by
RAY STEVENS

Moderately fast

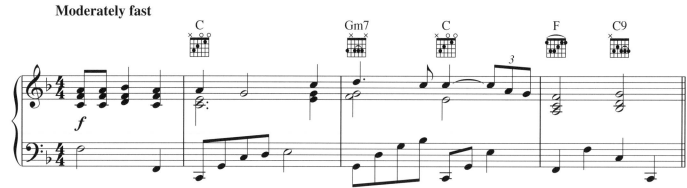

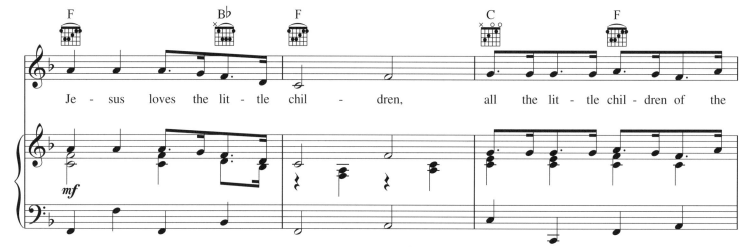

Je - sus loves the lit - tle chil - dren, all the lit - tle chil - dren of the world. Red and yel - low, black, and white, they are pre - cious in His sight, Je - sus

loves the lit - tle chil - dren of the world. _____ Ev - 'ry - thing is

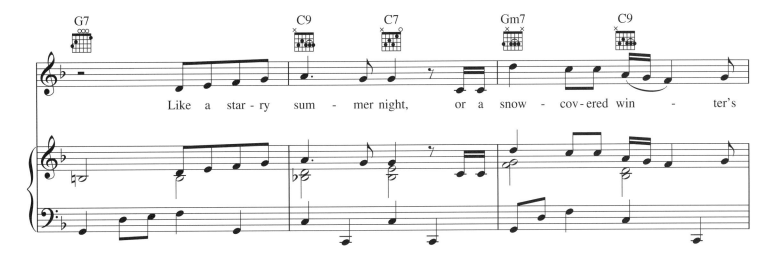

20

you know the world gets a lit - tle bit old - er.   It's time to re - al - ize

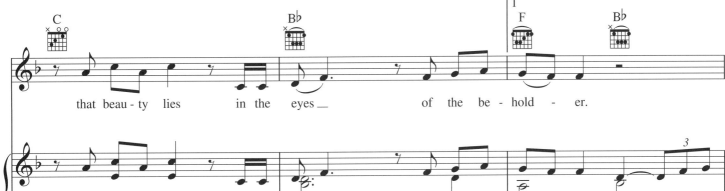

that beau - ty lies   in the eyes __   of the be - hold - er.

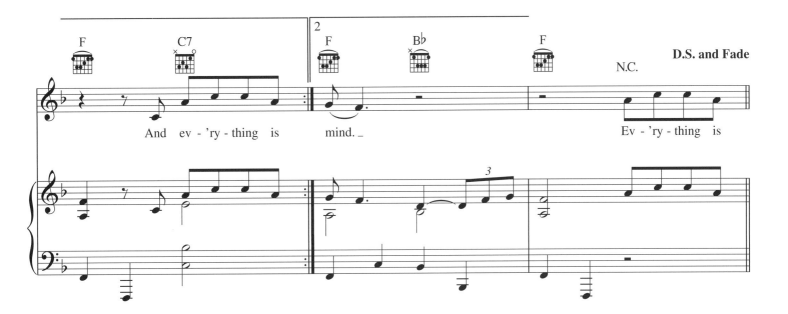

And ev - 'ry - thing is   mind. __   Ev - 'ry - thing is

Additional Lyrics

2. We shouldn't care about the length of his hair or the color of his skin,
Don't worry about what shows from without but the love that lies within,
We gonna get it all together now and everything gonna work out fine,
Just take a little time to look on the good side, my friend, and straighten it out in your mind.

GOD BLESS THE U.S.A.

Words and Music by
LEE GREENWOOD

stand up next to you and de-fend her still to-day.___ 'Cause there

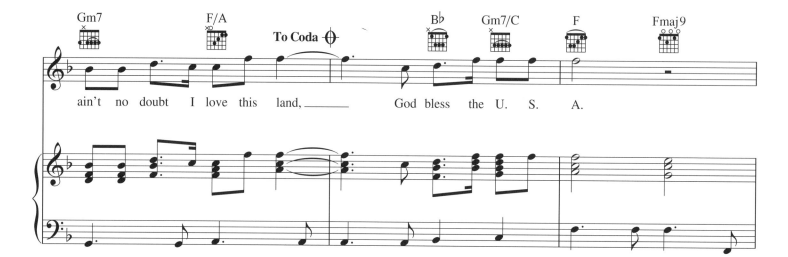

ain't no doubt I love this land,_____ God bless the U. S. A.

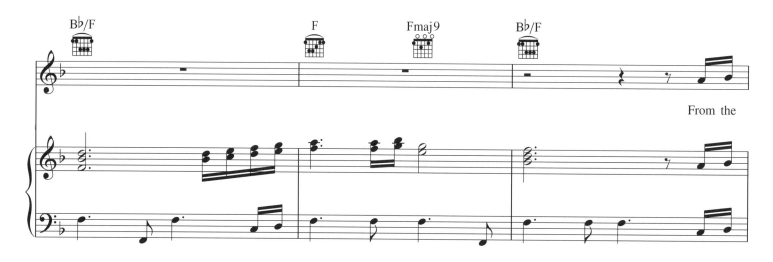

From the

lakes of Min-ne-so-ta, to the hills of Ten-nes-see,___ a-cross the plains_ of Tex-as, from

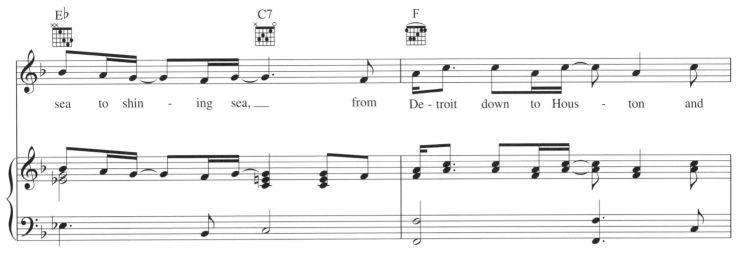

sea to shin - ing sea, ___ from De - troit down to Hous - ton and

New York to L. A., well, there's pride in ev - 'ry A - mer - i - can heart, and it's

time to stand and say ___ that I'm

D.S. al Coda

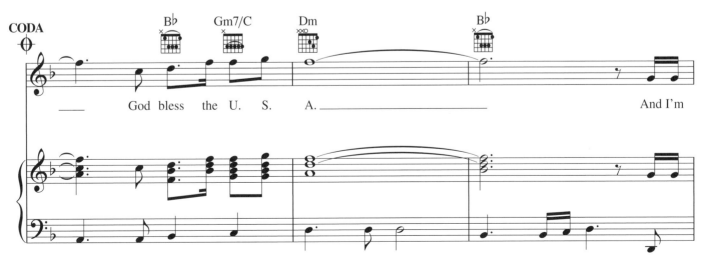

CODA

___ God bless the U. S. A. ___ And I'm

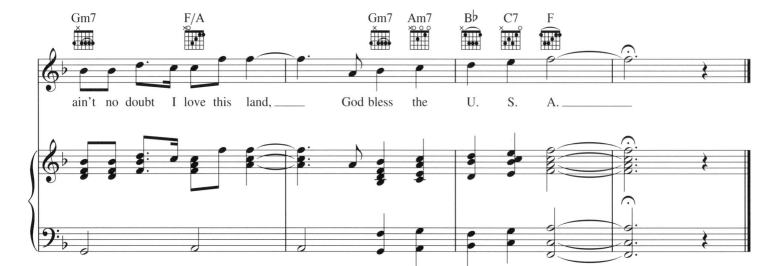

HE

Words by RICHARD MULLEN
Music by JACK RICHARDS

Moderately slow

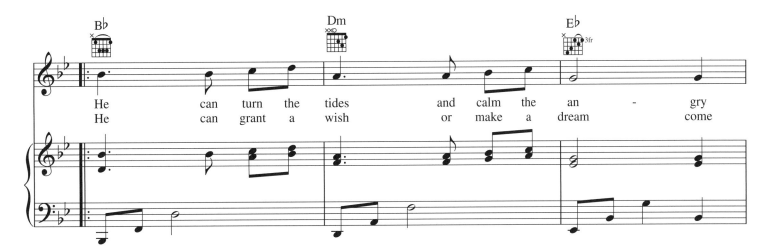

He can turn the tides and calm the an - gry
He can grant a wish or make a dream come

sea; He a - lone de - cides who writes a
true, He can paint the clouds and turn the

sym - pho - ny; He lights ev - 'ry
gray to blue; He a - lone knows

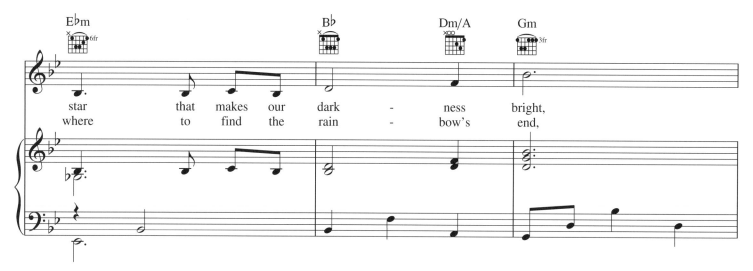

star that makes our dark - ness bright,
where to find the rain - bow's end,

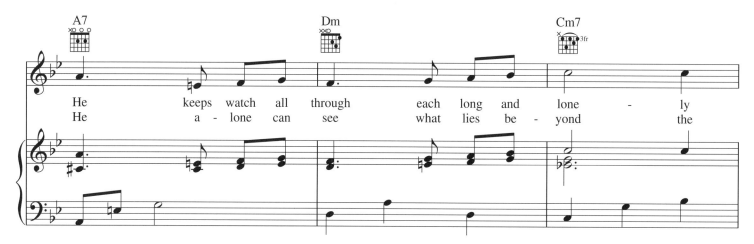

He keeps watch all through each long and lone - ly
He a - lone can see what lies be - yond the

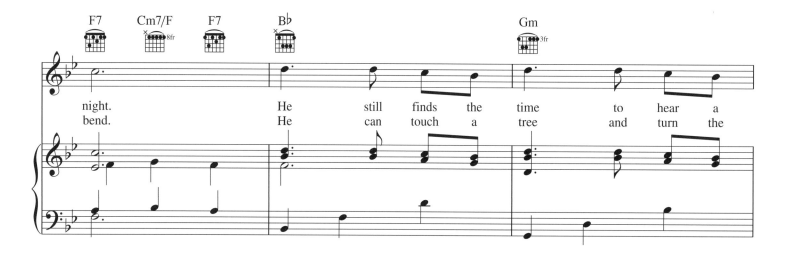

night. He still finds the time to hear a
bend. He can touch a tree and turn the

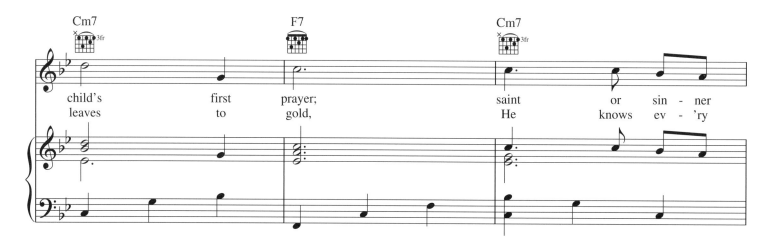

child's first prayer; saint or sin - ner
leaves to gold, He knows ev - 'ry

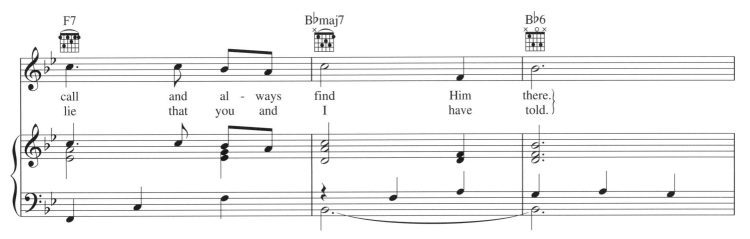

call and al - ways find Him there.}
lie that you and I have told.}

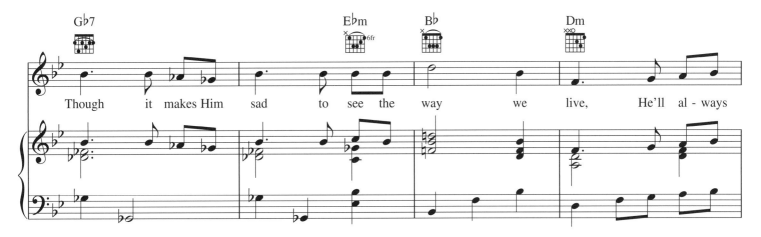

Though it makes Him sad to see the way we live, He'll al - ways

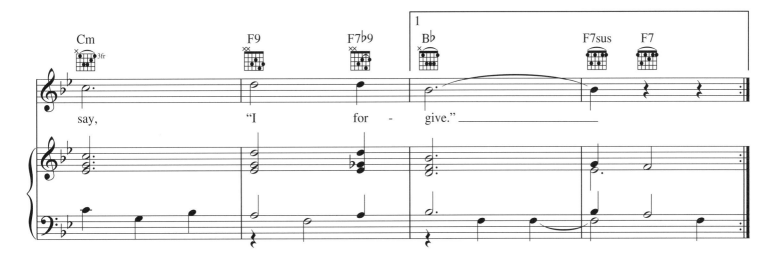

say, "I for - give." _____

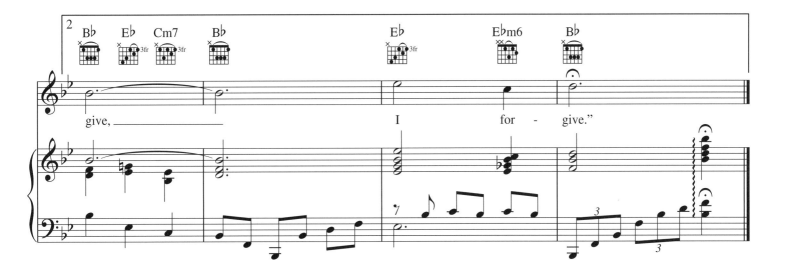

give, _____ I for - give."

I AM A MAN OF CONSTANT SORROW

featured in O BROTHER, WHERE ART THOU?

Words and Music by
CARTER STANLEY

Moderately fast Country

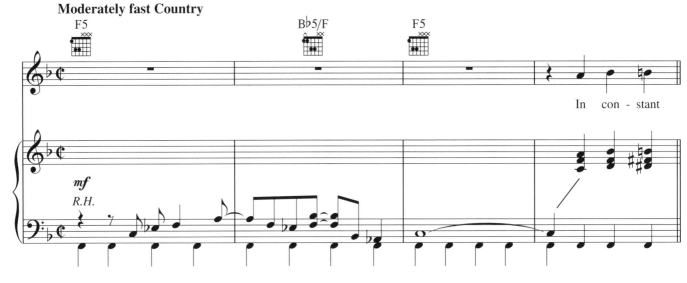

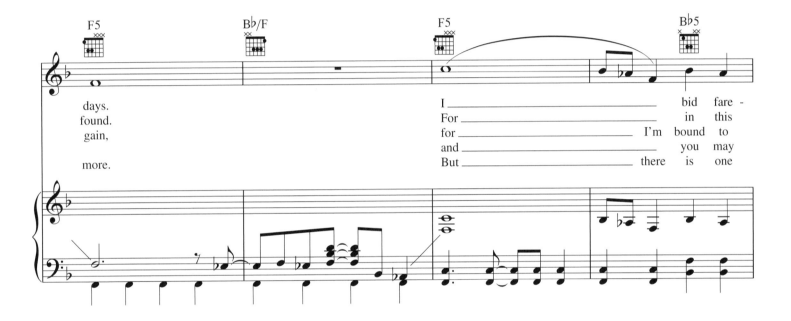

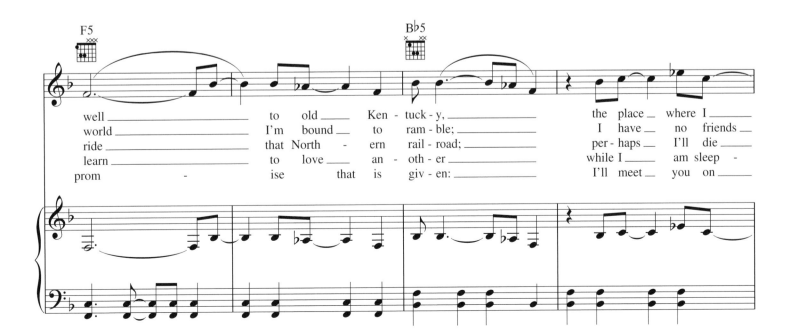

was born and raised.
to help me now.
up - on this train.
ing in my grave.
God's gold - en shore.

The place where
He has no
Per - haps he'll
While he is
He'll meet you

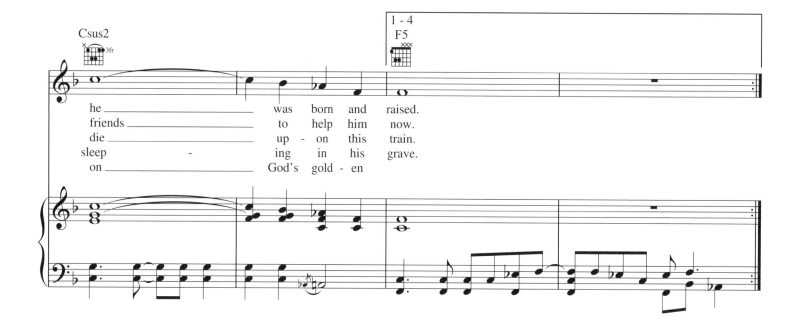

he ____ was born and raised.
friends ____ to help him now.
die ____ up - on this train.
sleep - ing in his grave.
on ____ God's gold - en

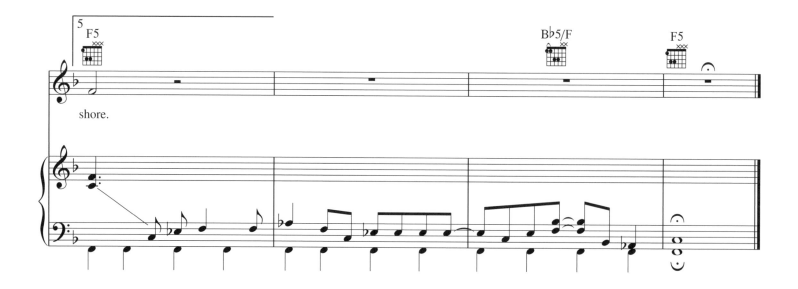

shore.

I AM A PILGRIM

Words and Music by
MERLE TRAVIS

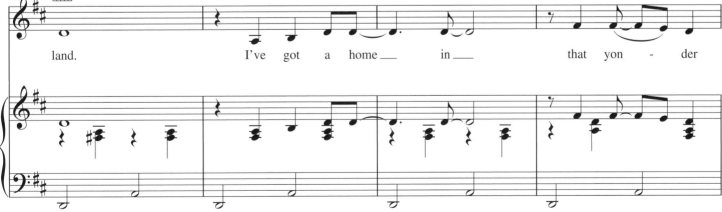

To Coda

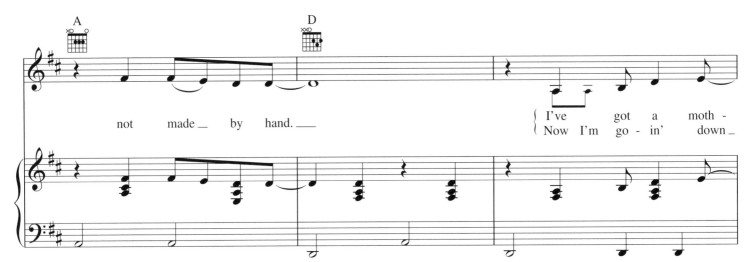

I BELIEVE

Words and Music by ERVIN DRAKE, IRVIN GRAHAM,
JIMMY SHIRL and AL STILLMAN

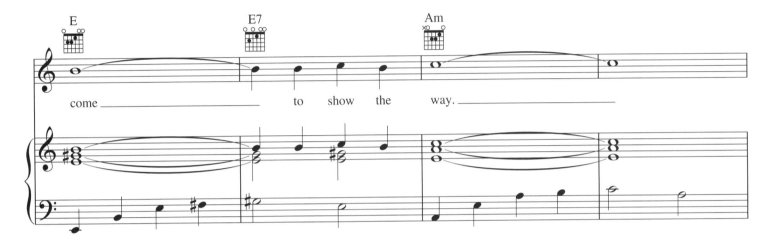

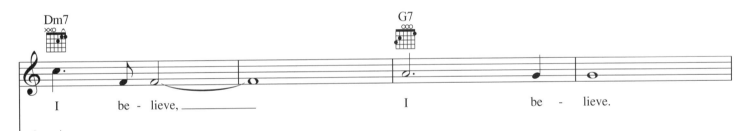

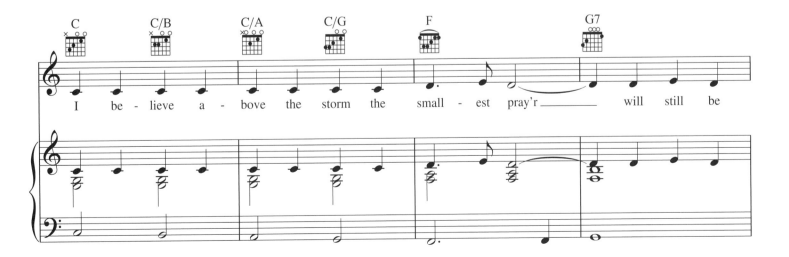

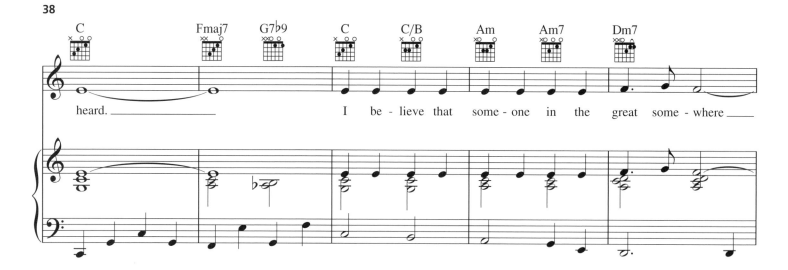

heard. _____ I be - lieve that some - one in the great some - where ____

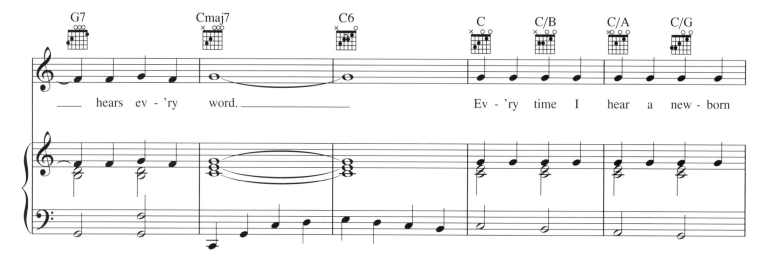

____ hears ev - 'ry word. _____ Ev - 'ry time I hear a new - born

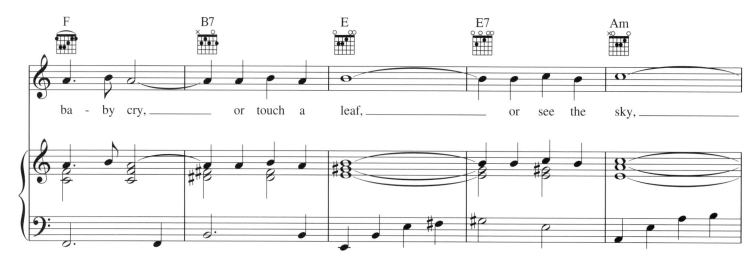

ba - by cry, _____ or touch a leaf, _____ or see the sky, _____

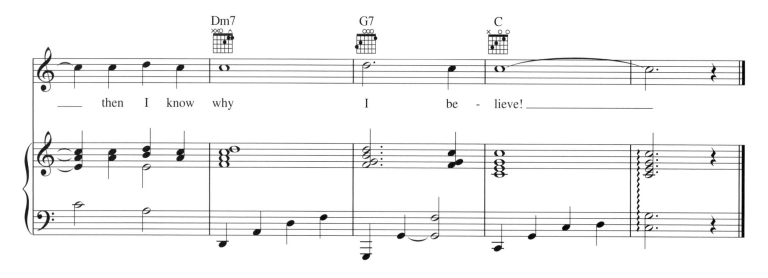

____ then I know why I be - lieve! _____

I SAW THE LIGHT

Words and Music by
HANK WILLIAMS

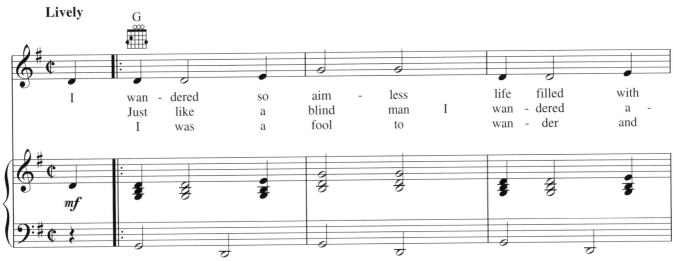

Lively

I wan - dered so aim - less life filled with
Just like a blind man I wan - dered a -
I was a fool to wan - der and

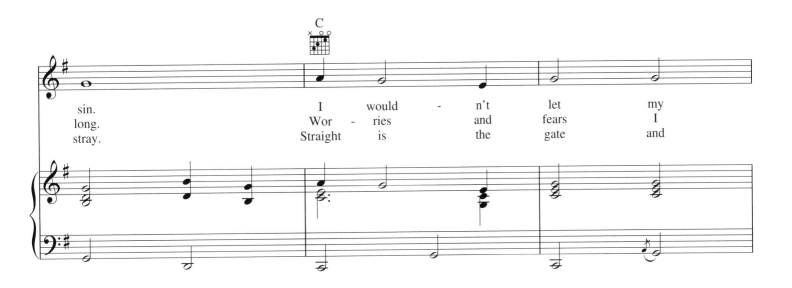

sin. I would - n't let my
long. Wor - ries and fears I
stray. Straight is the gate and

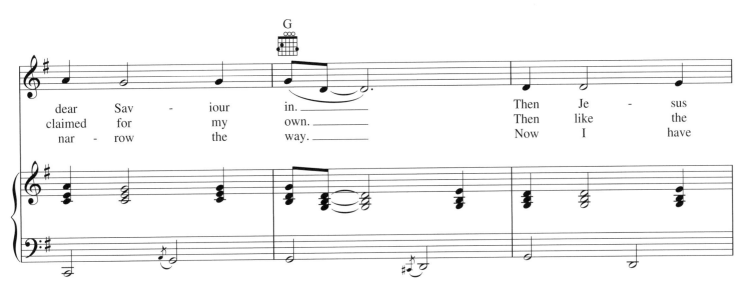

dear Sav - iour in. Then Je - sus
claimed for my own. Then like the
nar - row the way. Now I have

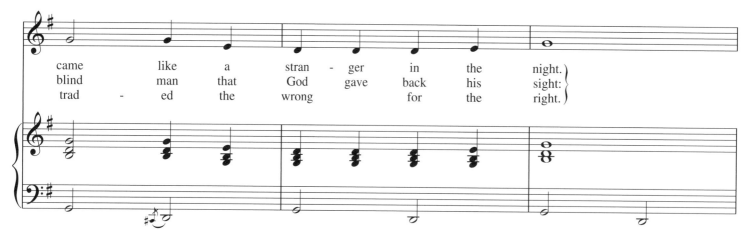

came like a stran - ger in the night.
blind man that God gave back his sight:
trad - ed the wrong for the right.

Praise the Lord, _____ I saw the

G

light. I saw the

light. _____ I saw the light. _____

I'LL TAKE YOU THERE

Words and Music by
ALVERTIS ISBELL

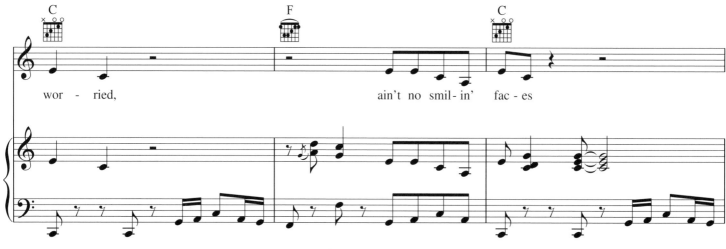

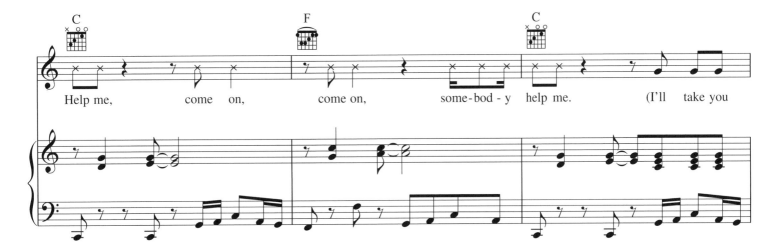

there.)
Mer-cy. (I'll take you there.)

Let me take you there. (I'll take you there.)
Let me take you. (I'll take you

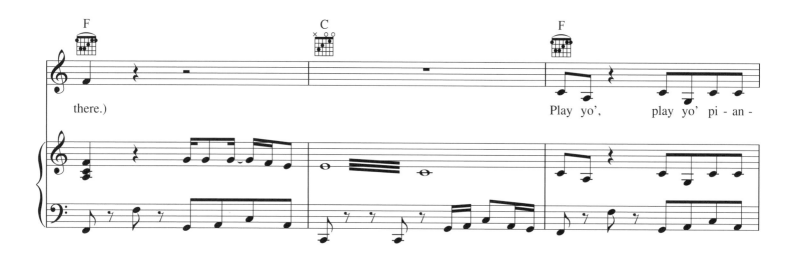

there.)
Play yo', play yo' pi-an-

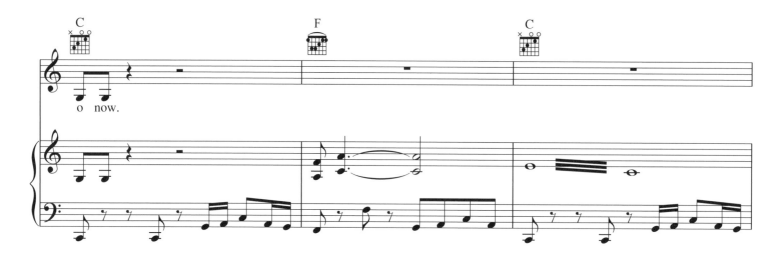

o now.

Come on now. Play on it, play on it.

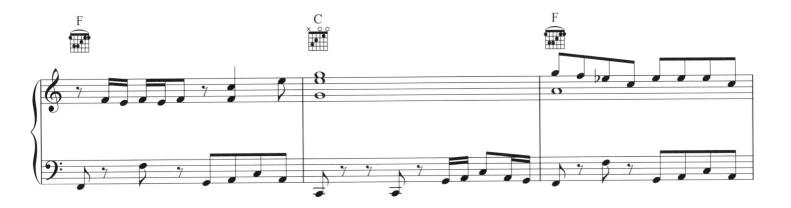

Ba - by, lit - tle ba - by,

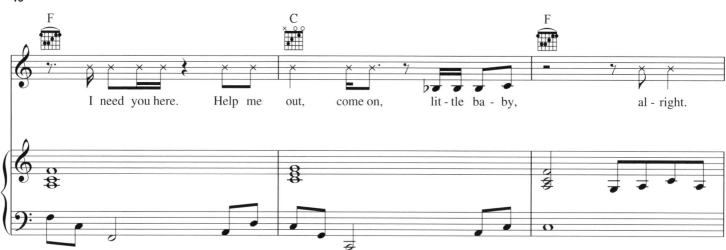

I need you here. Help me out, come on, lit-tle ba-by, al-right.

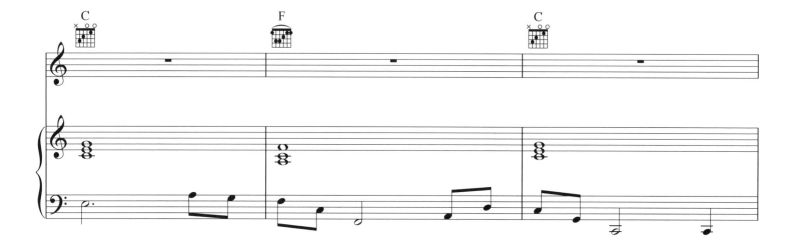

I, oh, I, I know a

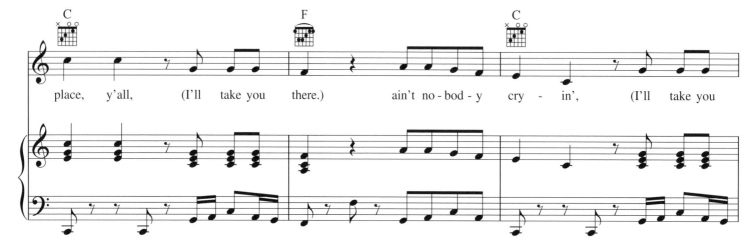

place, y'all, (I'll take you there.) ain't no-bod-y cry-in', (I'll take you

there.) ain't no-bod-y wor-ried, (I'll take you there.) no smil-in'

fac - es, (I'll take you there.) ly - in' to the

rac - es. (I'll take you there.)

Repeat and Fade
(Vocal ad lib.)

Optional Ending

(I'll take you there.)

IT IS NO SECRET
(What God Can Do)

Words and Music by
STUART HAMBLEN

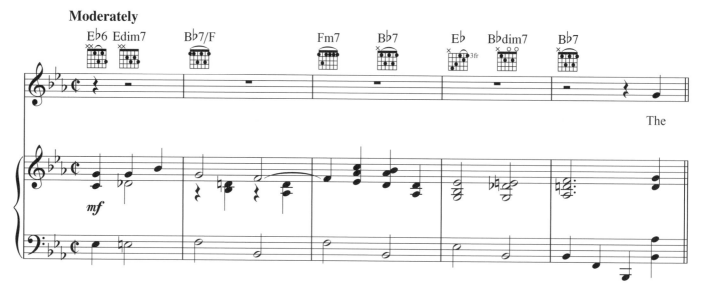

The

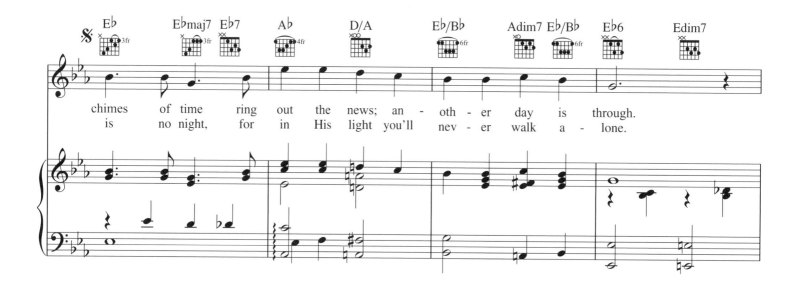

chimes of time ring out the news; an- oth- er day is through.
is no night, for in His light you'll nev- er walk a - lone.

Some - one slipped and fell. Was that some - one you? You
Al - ways feel at home wher - ev - er you may roam. There

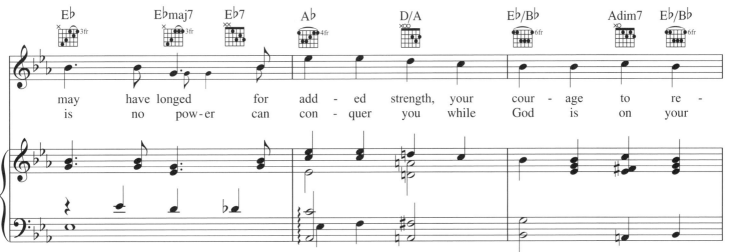

may have longed for add - ed strength, your cour - age to re -
is no pow-er can con - quer you while God is on your

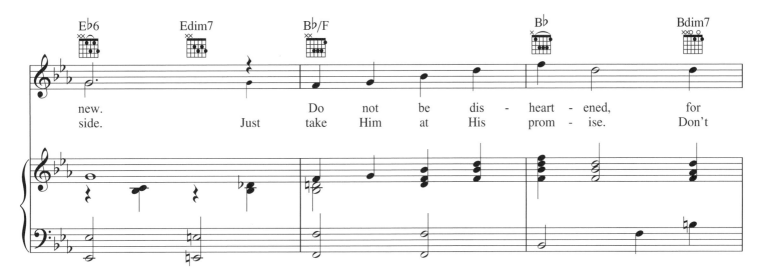

new. Just Do take Him at dis - heart - ened, for
side. Do take Him at His prom - ise. Don't

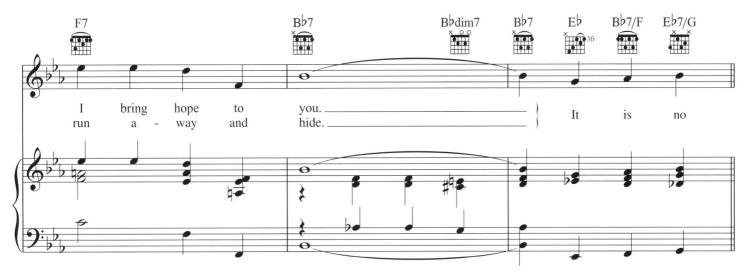

I bring hope to you. It is no
run a - way and hide.

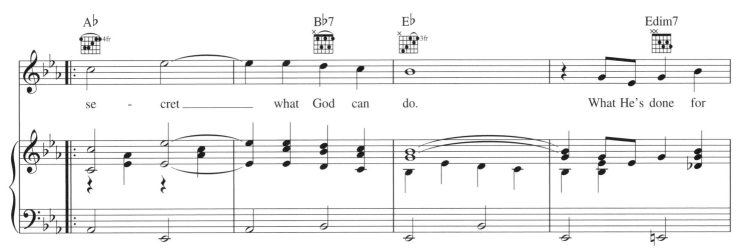

se - cret what God can do. What He's done for

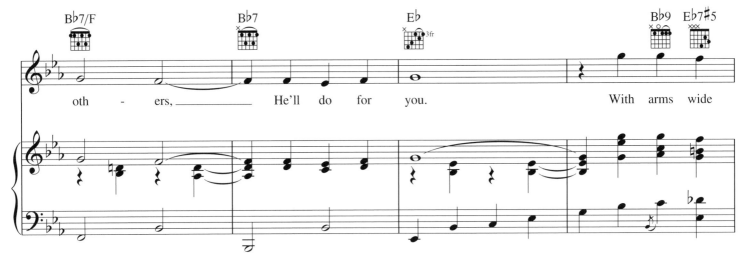

oth - ers, _____ He'll do for you. With arms wide

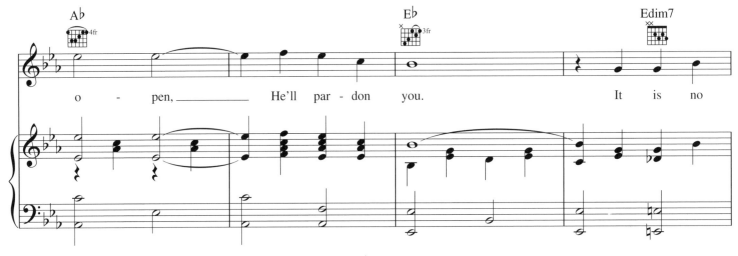

o - pen, _____ He'll par - don you. It is no

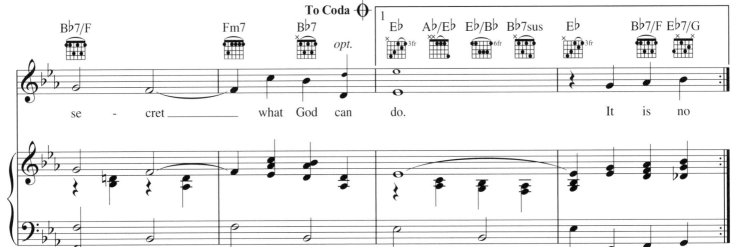

se - cret _____ what God can do. It is no

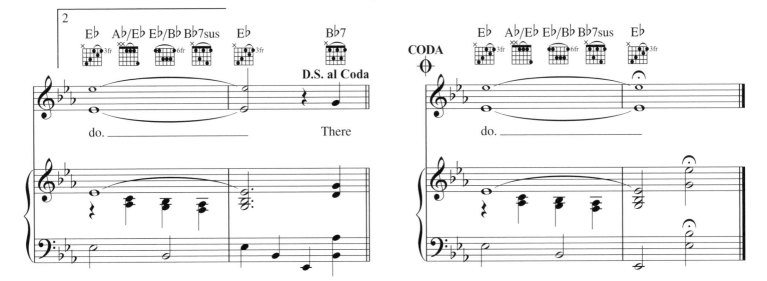

do. _____ There

do. _____

JESUS, HE LOVES ME

featured in the Epic Mini-Series JESUS

Arrangement by
EDWIN McCAIN

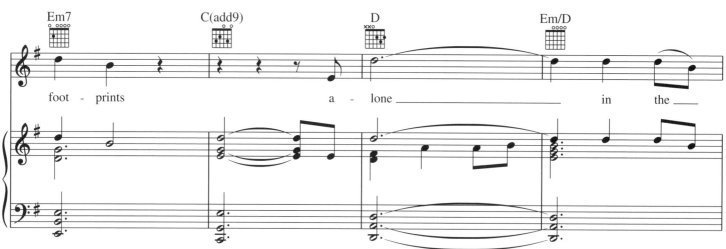

foot - prints   a - lone _____ in the ____

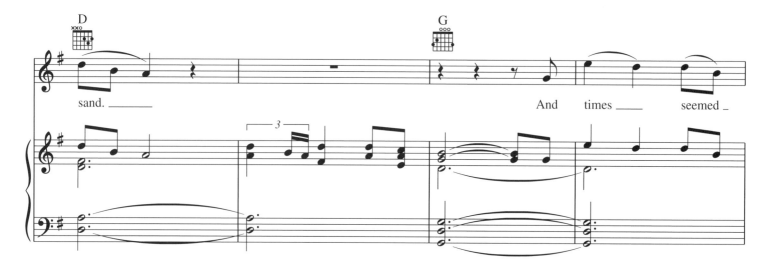

sand. _____   And times _____ seemed _

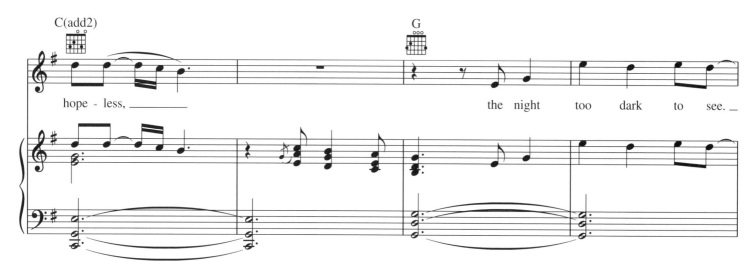

hope - less, _____   the night too dark to see. _

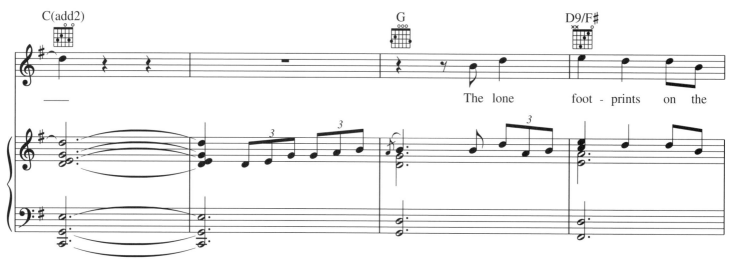

_____ The lone foot - prints on the

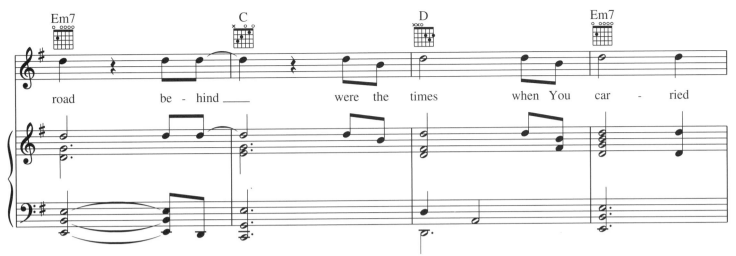

road be - hind _____ were the times when You car - ried

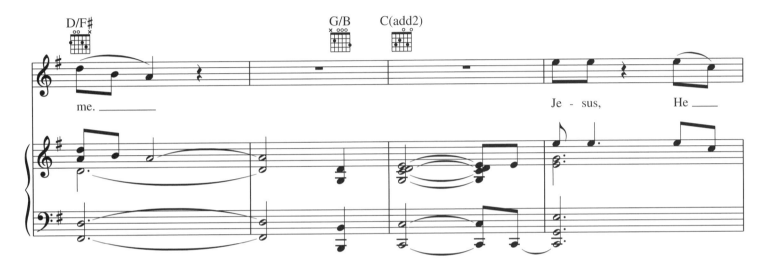

me. _____ Je - sus, He _____

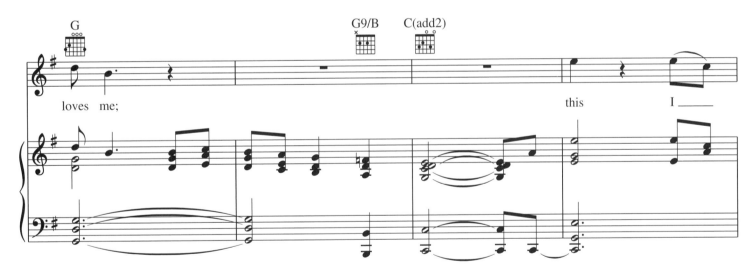

loves me; this I _____ know.

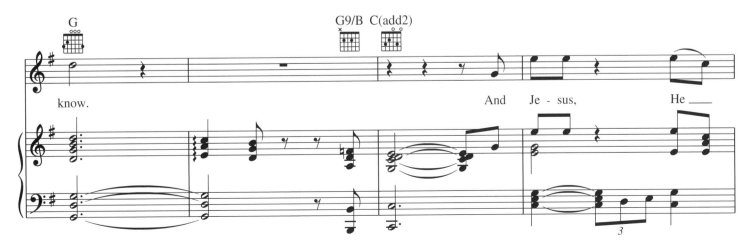

And Je - sus, He _____

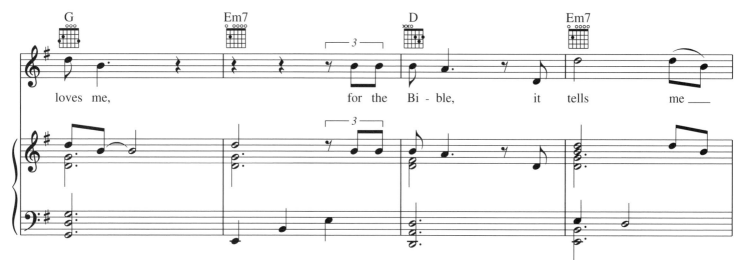

loves me, for the Bi - ble, it tells me

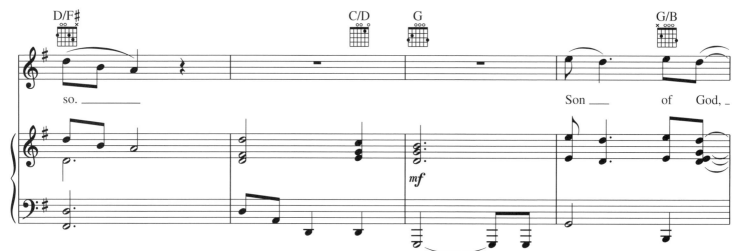

so. Son of God,

our Sav - ior and

King, You're tak-ing a - way the

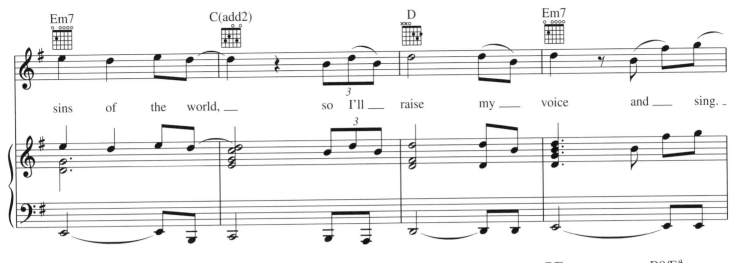

sins of the world, ___ so I'll ___ raise my ___ voice and ___ sing. ___

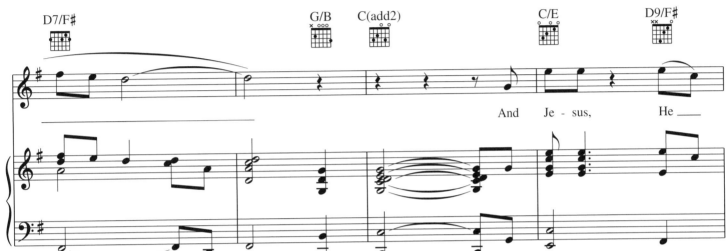

And Je - sus, He ___

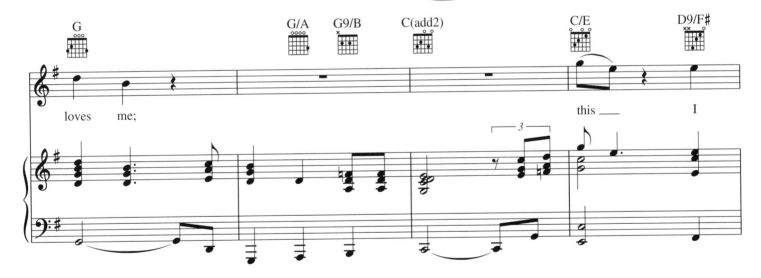

loves me; this ___ I

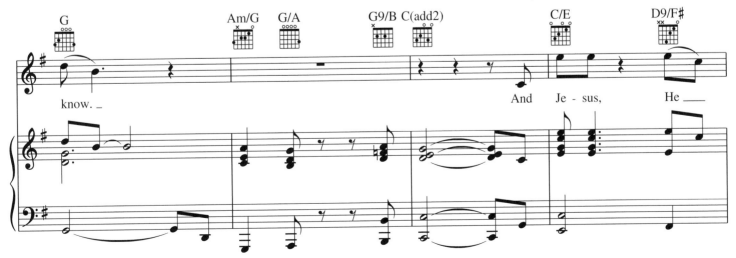

know. ___ And Je - sus, He ___

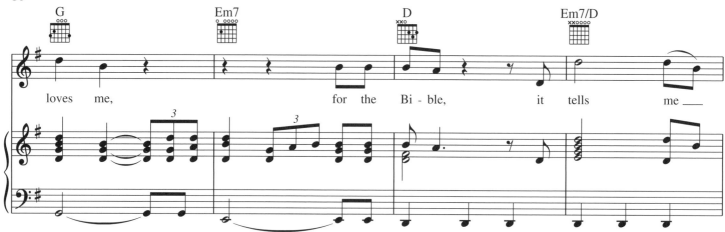

loves me, _____ for the Bi - ble, it tells me _____

so. _____ Now I've held the hand of the ___

dev - il _____ at ____ the cross - roads of my faith, _

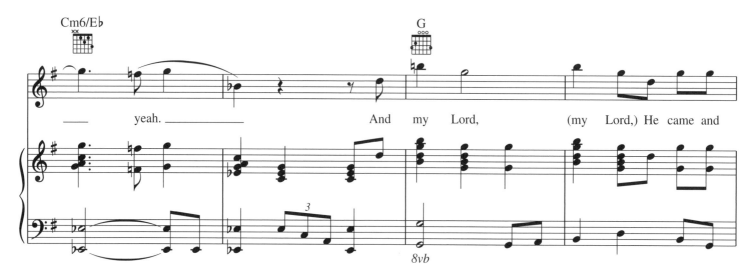

_____ yeah. _____ And my Lord, (my Lord,) He came and

JESUS IS JUST ALRIGHT

Words and Music by
ARTHUR REYNOLDS

Je - sus is just __ al - right __ with me. __

Je - sus is just __ al - right, __ whoa yeah. __ Je - sus is just __ al - right __

__ with me. __ Je - sus is just __ al - right. __

I don't care ___ what they ___ may {say. ___ / know. _}

I don't care ___ {what / where} they ___ may {do. ___ / go. ___} I don't care ___ what they ___

___ may {say. ___ / know. _} Je - sus is just ___ al - right, oh yeah. _

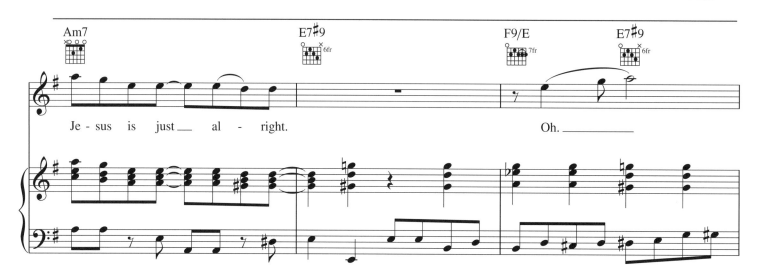

Je - sus is just ___ al - right. Oh. ___

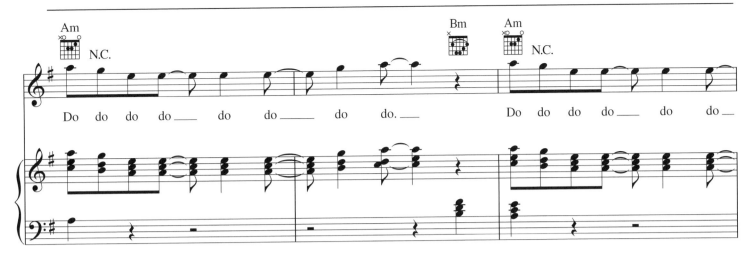

Do do do do __ do do __ do do. __

Do do do do __ do do __

__ do do. __ Do do do do __ do do __ do do. __

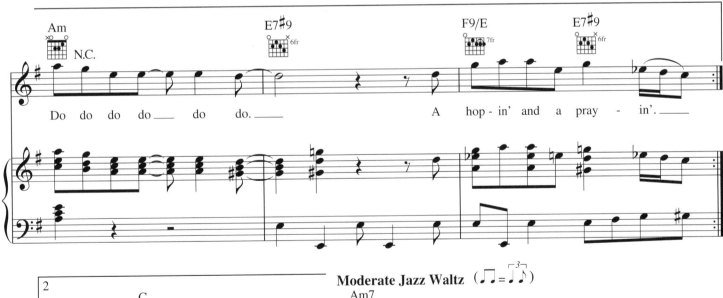

Do do do do __ do do. __ A hop-in' and a pray-in'. __

Moderate Jazz Waltz

oh yeah. __

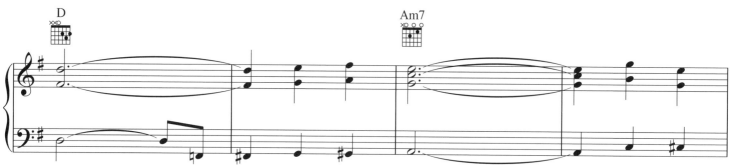

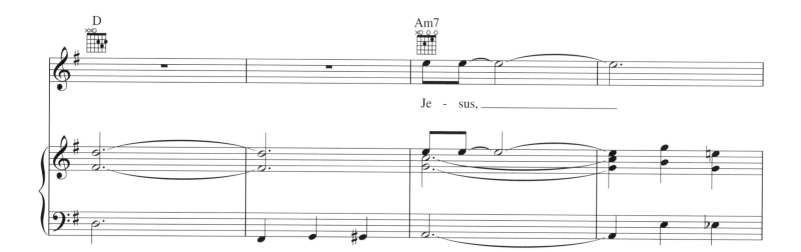

Je - sus, _____

he's my   friend. _____
Guitar solo ad lib.

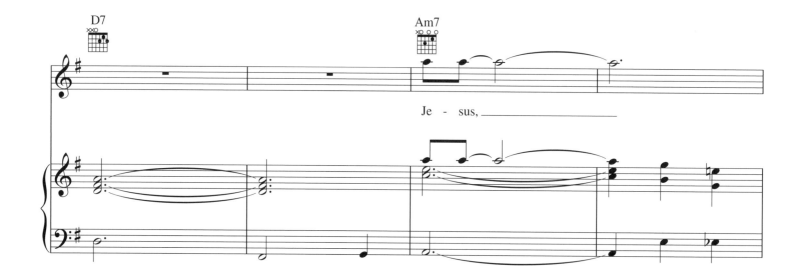

Je - sus, _____

well, he's my _____ friend. _____

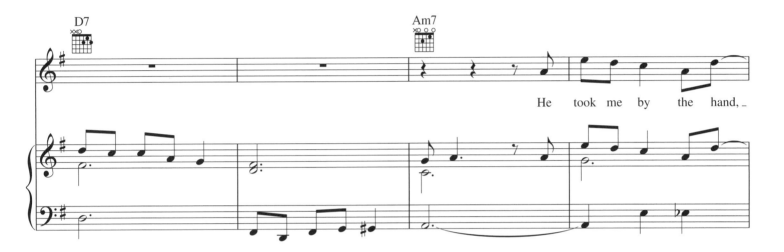

He took me by the hand, _

led me far _____

_ from this land. _____ Je - sus, _____

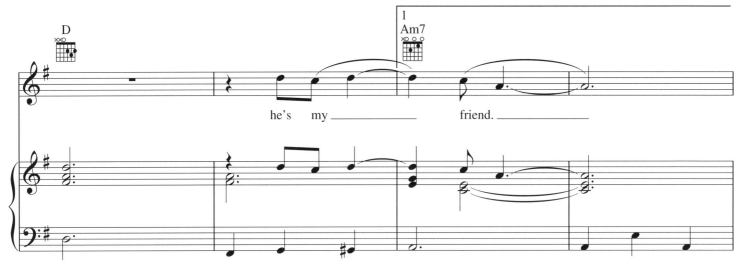

he's my _____ friend. _____

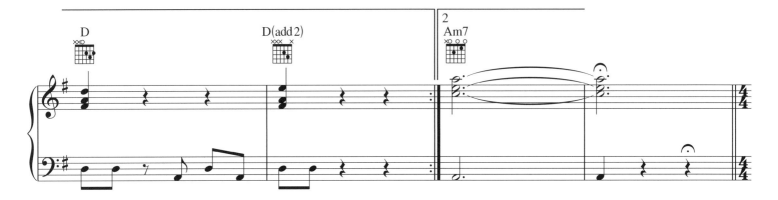

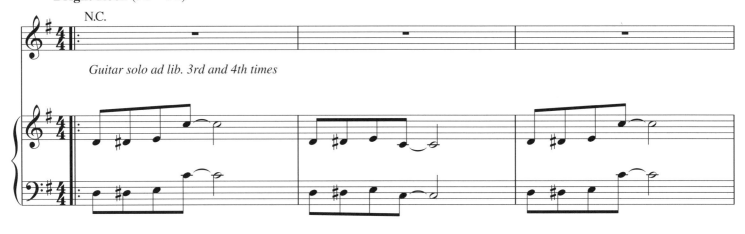

Bright Rock (♪♪ = ♪♪)

N.C.

Guitar solo ad lib. 3rd and 4th times

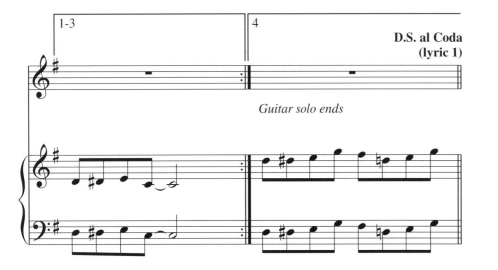

D.S. al Coda
(lyric 1)

Guitar solo ends

CODA

oh yeah. _

KNEEL AT THE FEET OF JESUS

Words and Music by
WILLIE NELSON

Upbeat Country feel

Well, I guess I've been hang-ing a-round too long; it's just a-bout time I was mov-ing a-long. But I'm a-gon-na

kneel at the feet of Je-sus in the morn-ing.

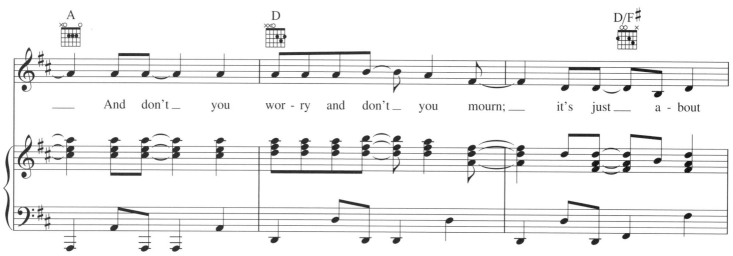

And don't_ you wor-ry and don't_ you mourn;_ it's just_ a-bout

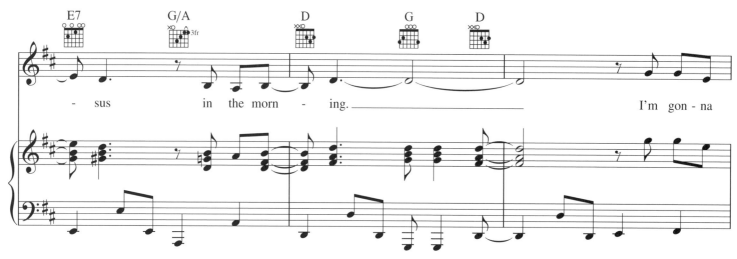

time _ I was mov-ing a-long._ But I'm a-gon-na kneel at the feet of Je-

-sus in the morn - ing._____ I'm gon-na

kneel at the feet of Je - sus_____ in the morn - ing._

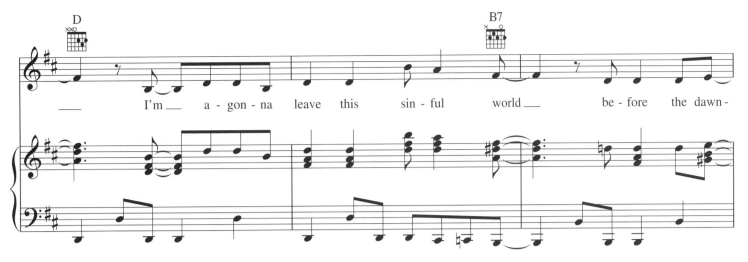

I'm_ a-gon-na leave this sin-ful world _ be-fore the dawn-

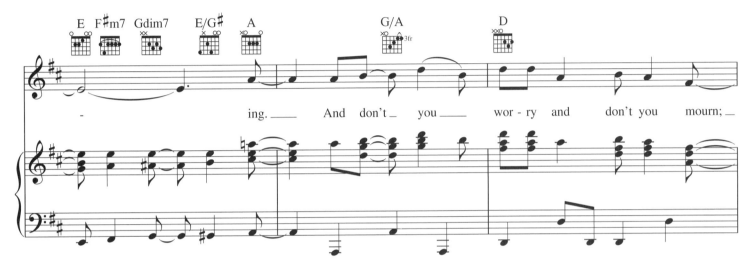

-ing. _ And don't_ you _ wor-ry and don't you mourn; _

_ it's just_ a-bout time_ I was mov-ing a-long. _ But I'm a-gon-na

To Coda ⊕

kneel at the feet of Je - sus _ in the morn - ing. _

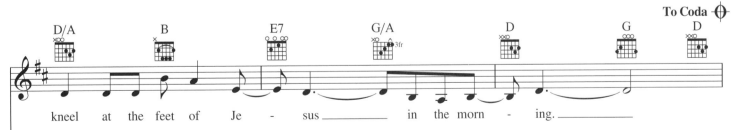

G7 G#dim7 D/A D

B7 D D/F# G G#dim7 G/A

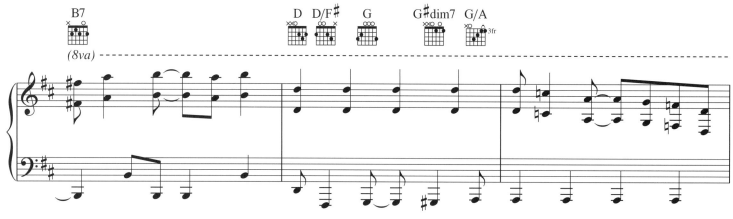

D G

G#dim7 D/A B7 E7 A

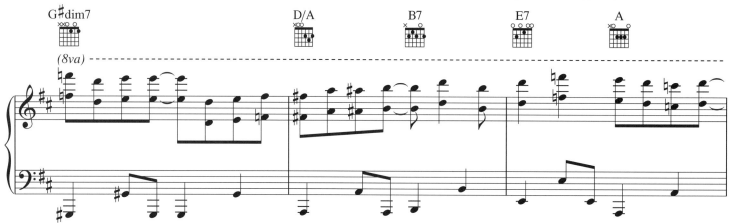

Just one thing be-fore you car-ry me a-way: __

__ don't you bur-y me __ deep, __ 'cause I ain't gon-na stay. __ I'm __ a-gon-na

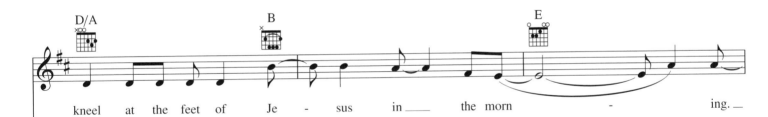

kneel at the feet of Je - sus in __ the morn - - - ing. __

__ Just a lit-tle bit of dirt and a lit-tle bit of grav-el. Don't you weigh me down, __

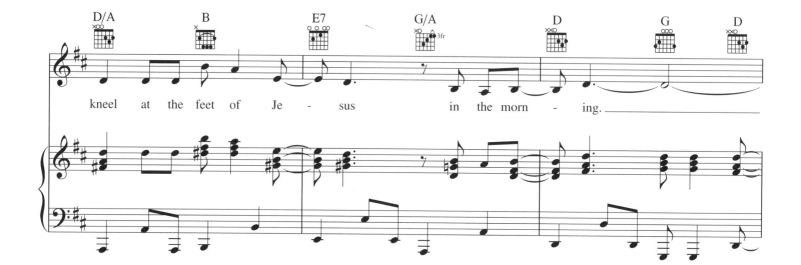

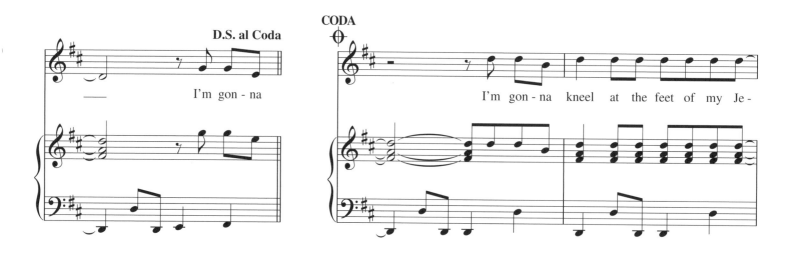

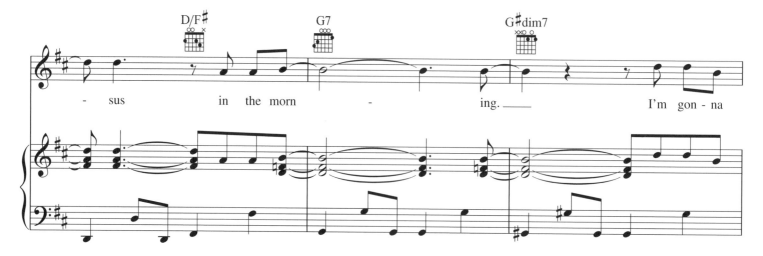

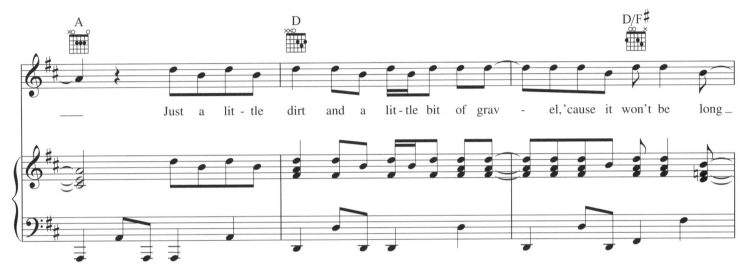

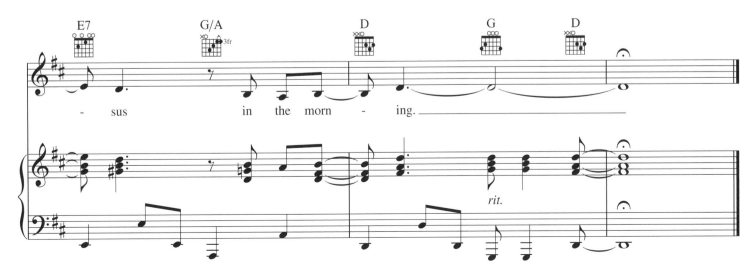

LONG BLACK TRAIN

Words and Music by
JOSH TURNER

Moderate Country Gospel

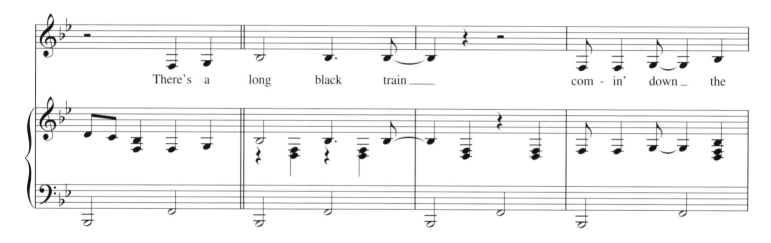

There's a long black train ____ com - in' down ____ the

line, feed - in' off ____ the souls ____ that are lost ____ and

cry - in'. Rails of ____ sin, ____ on - ly e - vil re - mains. ____

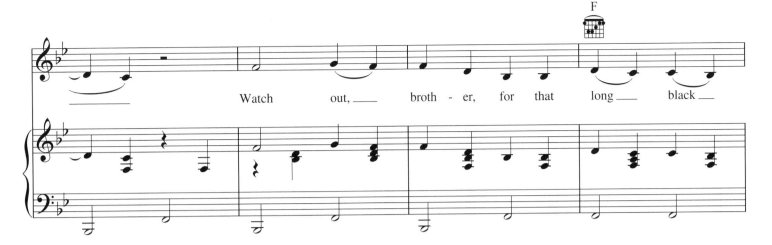

Watch out, ___ broth - er, for that long ___ black ___

train.

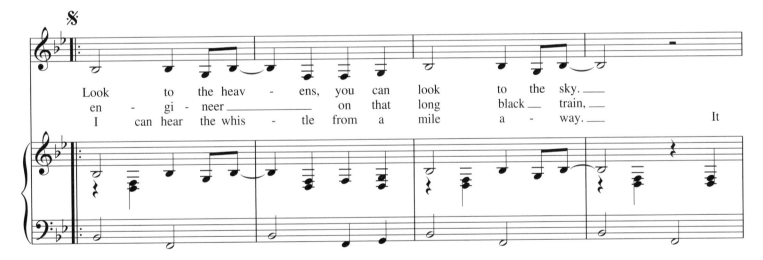

Look to the heav - ens, you can look to the sky. ___
en - gi - neer ___ on that long black ___ train, ___
I can hear the whis - tle from a mile a - way. ___ It

You can find ___ re-demp - tion star - in' back ___ in - to ___ your eyes. ___
mak - in' ___ you won - der if the ride ___ is worth the pain. ___
sounds ___ so ___ good, ___ but I ___ must stay a - way. ___ That

There is pro-tec — tion and there's peace __ the same __
He's just a-wait — in' on your heart __ to say, __
train is a beau — ty, mak-in' ev-'ry-bod — y stare. __ But its

burn — in' __ your tick-et for that long __ black __ train.
"Let me __ ride __ on that long __ black __ train."
on — ly des-ti — na-tion is the mid-dle of no — where.

'Cause there's
But you know there's } vic — t'ry _____ in the Lord, __ I
But you know there's

say. __ Vic — t'ry _____ in the Lord.

Cling to ___ the Fa - ther and His Ho - ly

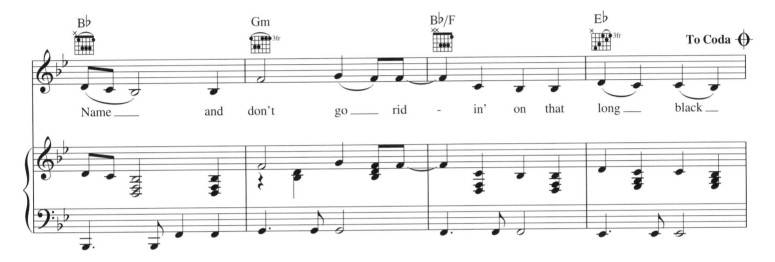

Name ___ and don't go ___ rid - in' on that long ___ black ___

1

train. There's an

2

train.

D.S. al Coda

Well,

CODA

train.   I say cling   to ___ the Fa -

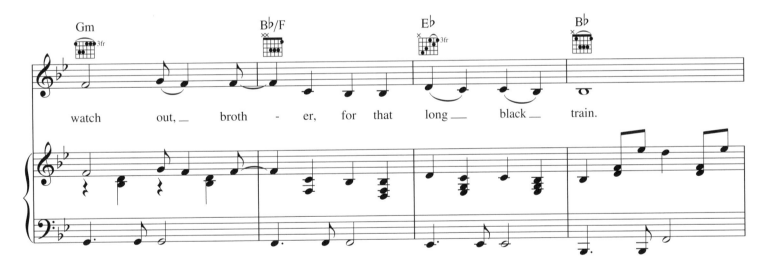

OVER THE NEXT HILL WE'LL BE HOME

Words and Music by
JOHN R. CASH

By the way the land is lay-ing, I think
speed that we've been mak-ing, I would

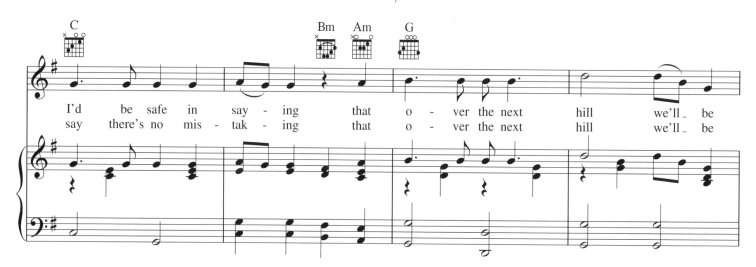

I'd be safe in say-ing that o-ver the next hill we'll be
say there's no mis-tak-ing that o-ver the next hill we'll be

home. _____ It's a straight and nar-row
home. _____ There's a place that we ___ are

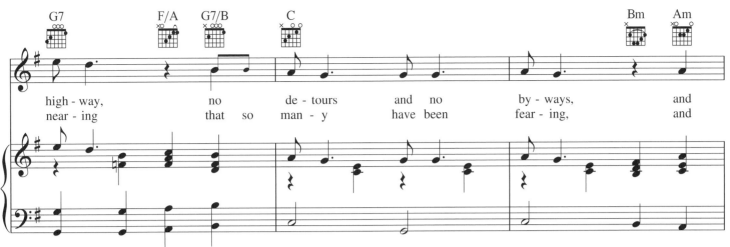

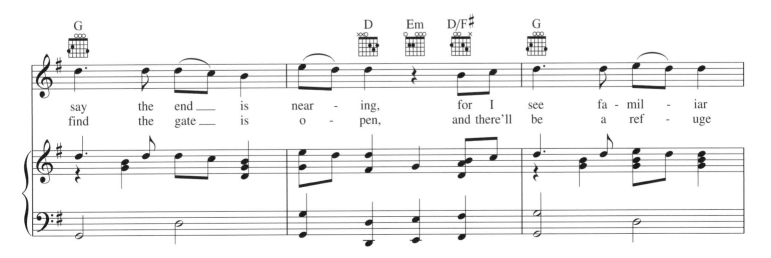

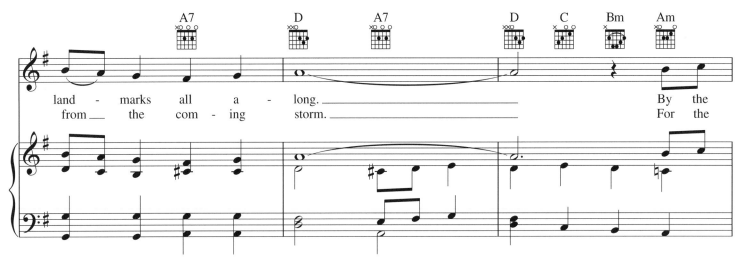

land - marks all a - long. _____ By the
from ___ the com - ing storm. _____ For the

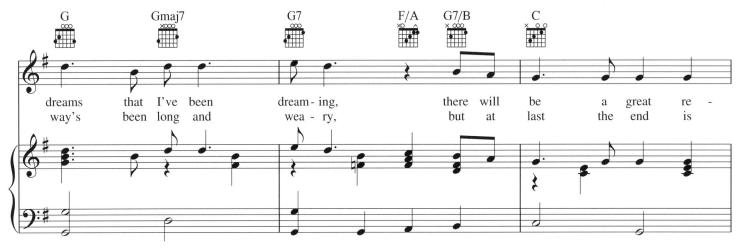

dreams that I've been dream - ing, there will be a great re -
way's been long and wea - ry, but at last the end is

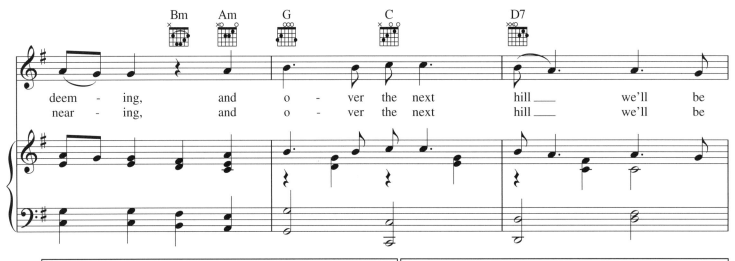

deem - ing, and o - ver the next hill ___ we'll be
near - ing, and o - ver the next hill ___ we'll be

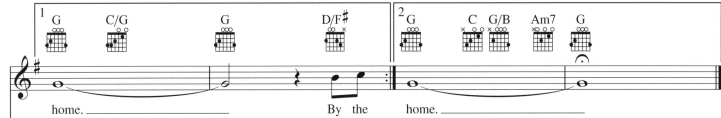

home. _____ By the home. _____

PUT YOUR HAND IN THE HAND

Words and Music by
GENE MacLELLAN

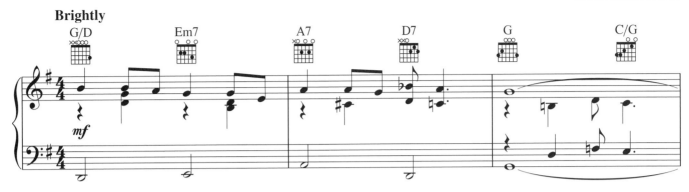

Put your hand in the hand of the man who stilled the wa-ter. ___

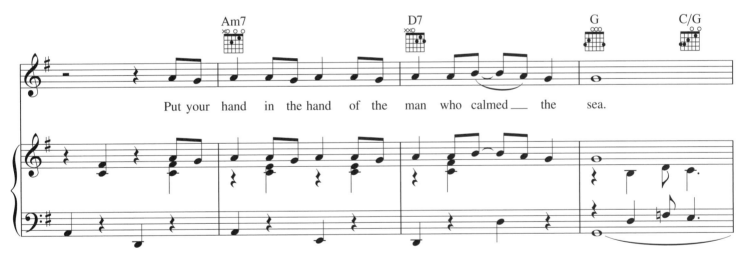

Put your hand in the hand of the man who calmed ___ the sea.

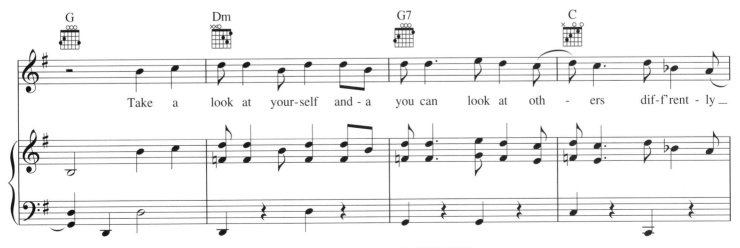

Take a look at your-self and - a you can look at oth - ers dif-f'rent-ly ___

by puttin' your hand in the hand of the man from a Gal-i-lee.

Ev-'ry time I look in-to the Ho-ly book I wan-na trem-ble
Ma-ma taught me how to pray be-fore I reached the age of sev-en,

when I read a-bout the part where a car-pen-ter cleared the
and when I'm down on my knees, that's-a when I'm close to

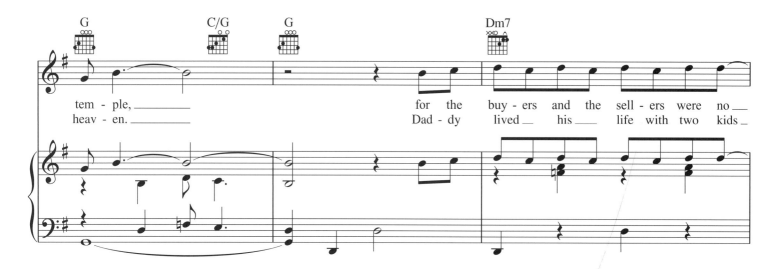

tem-ple, for the buy-ers and the sell-ers were no
heav-en. Dad-dy lived his life with two kids

PRETTY AMAZING GRACE

Words and Music by
NEIL DIAMOND

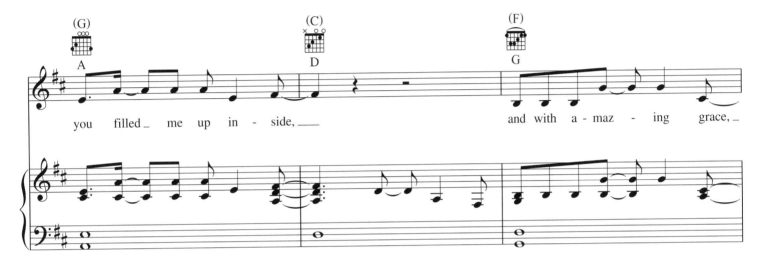

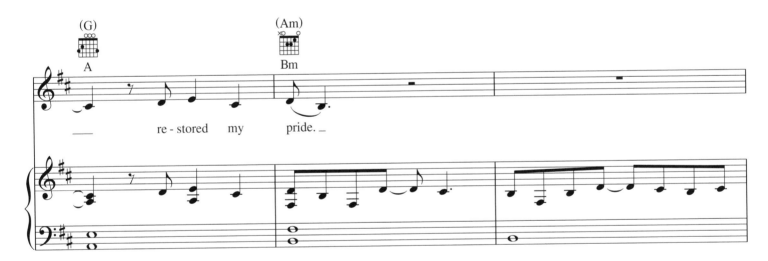

To Coda ⊕

truth I could _ be - lieve ___ in. You led me to that high - er place, _

___ showed _ me that love, and truth, and

hope, and grace were all I need - ed.

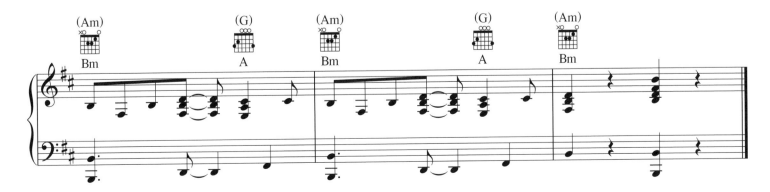

REACH OUT TO JESUS

Words and Music by
RALPH CARMICHAEL

Is your bur-den heav-y _____ as you bear it all a-

lone? _____ Does the road you trav-el _____ har-bor

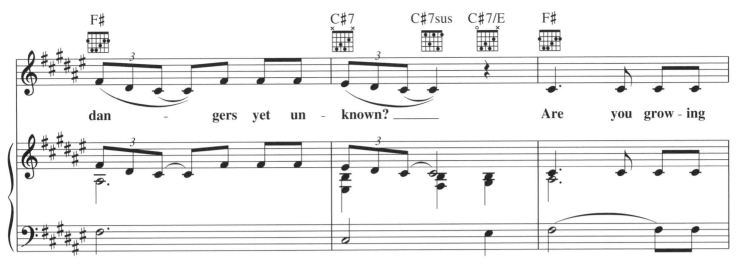

dan - gers yet un - known? _____ Are you grow - ing

wea - ry _____ in the strug - gle of it all? _____

Je - sus will help _ you _ when on His name you

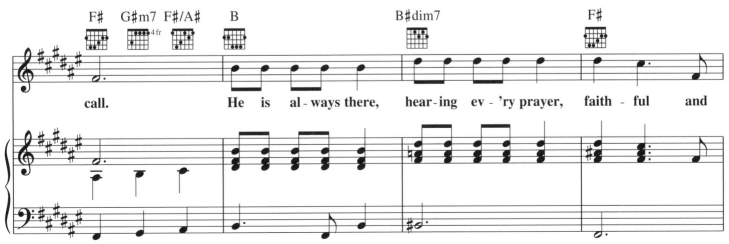

call. He is al - ways there, hear - ing ev - 'ry prayer, faith - ful and

SPIRIT IN THE SKY

Words and Music by
NORMAN GREENBAUM

Moderate Rock Shuffle

Play 3 times

When I die and they
Pre - pare your - self; ___ you
Nev - er been a sin - ner,

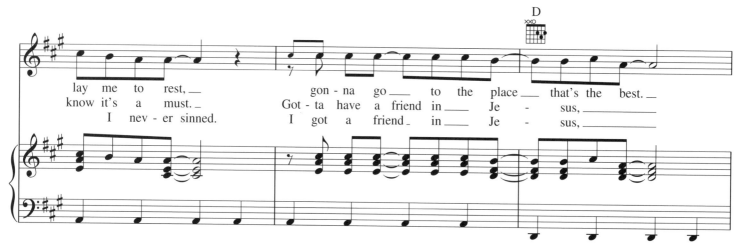

lay me to rest, ___ gon - na go ___ to the place ___ that's the best. ___
know it's a must. ___ Got - ta have a friend in ___ Je - sus, _____
I nev - er sinned. I got a friend _ in ___ Je - sus, _____

When I lay me down ___ to die, ___ go- in' up ___ to the Spir - it in the
so you know that when ___ you die, ___ He's gon- na rec - om-mend you to the
so you know that when ___ I die, ___ He's gon- na set me up ___ with the

sky.
Spir - it in the sky. ___ Go- in' up ___ to the Spir - it in the sky. ___
Spir - it in the sky. ___ He'll rec - om-mend you to the Spir - it in the sky. ___
He'll set me up ___ with the Spir - it in the sky.

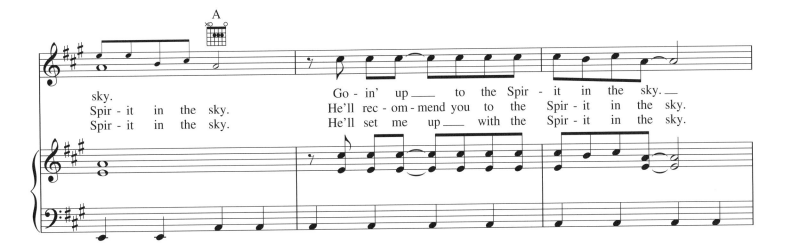

That's where I'm gon-na go ___ when I die. ___ When I die and they
That's where you're gon-na go ___ when you die. ___ When you die and they
That's where I'm gon-na go ___ when I die. ___ When I die and they

To Coda

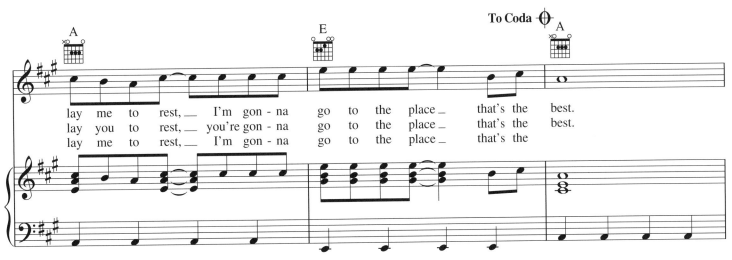

lay me to rest, ___ I'm gon - na go to the place ___ that's the best.
lay you to rest, ___ you're gon - na go to the place ___ that's the best.
lay me to rest, ___ I'm gon - na go to the place ___ that's the

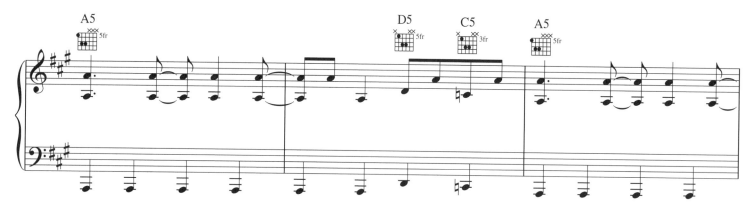

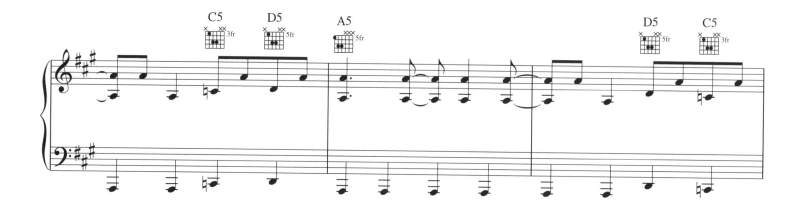

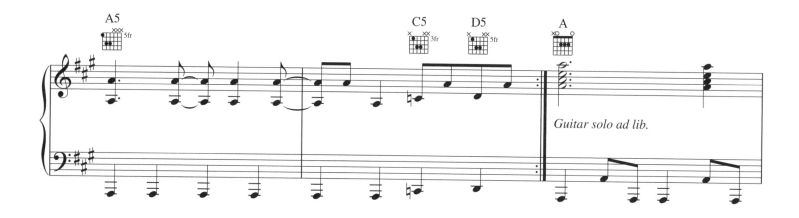

Guitar solo ad lib.

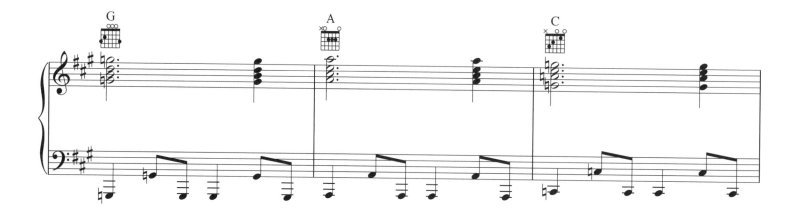

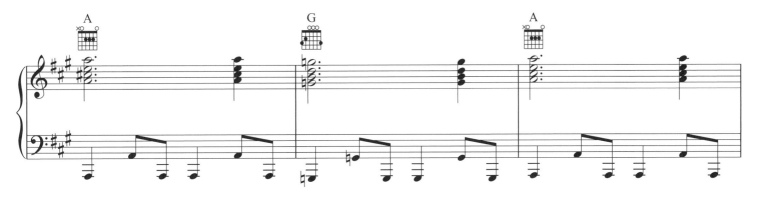

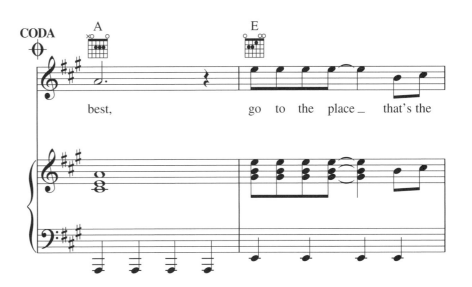

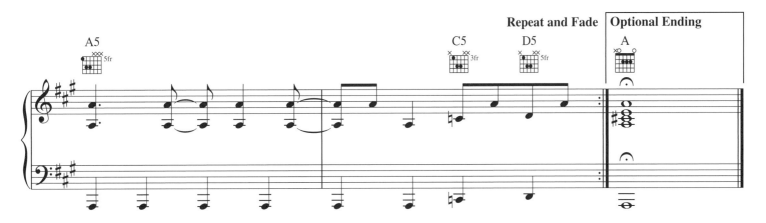

SUPERSTAR
from JESUS CHRIST SUPERSTAR

Words by TIM RICE
Music by ANDREW LLOYD WEBBER

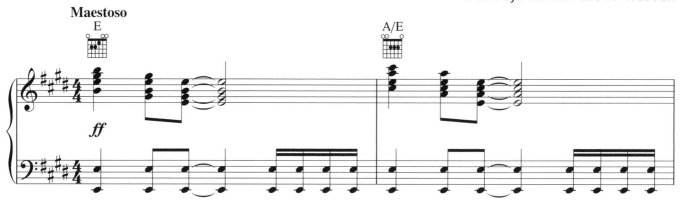

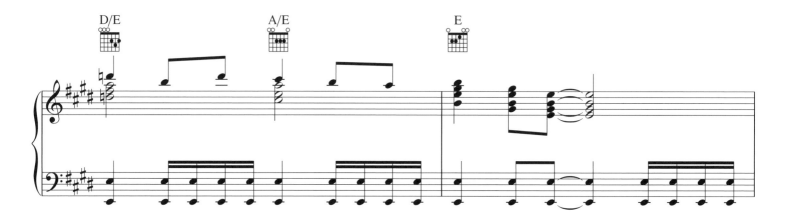

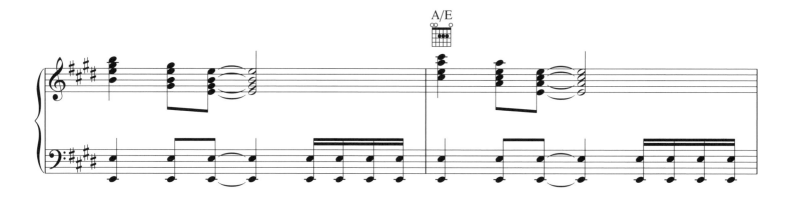

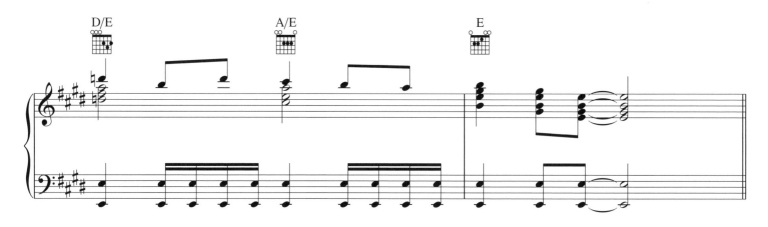

know) (I on-ly want to know now) (I on-ly want to
on - ly want to know, on - ly want to know, on - ly want to

know) (I on-ly want to know now.)
on - ly want to know, on - ly want to know.

Je - sus Christ, Je - sus Christ. Who are you? What have you

sa - cri - ficed? Je - sus Christ, Je - sus Christ.

Who are you? What have you sa - cri - ficed? _ Je - sus Christ, _

su - per - star, _ do you think you're what they say you are? _

Je - sus Christ, _ su - per - star, _ do you think you're what they

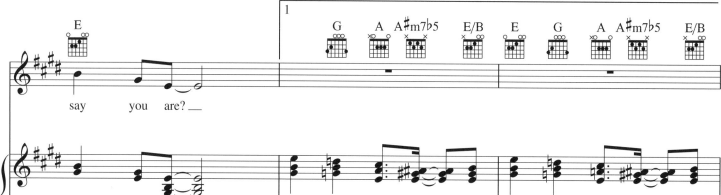

say you are? _

Je - sus Christ, _ su - per - star, _ do you think you're what they

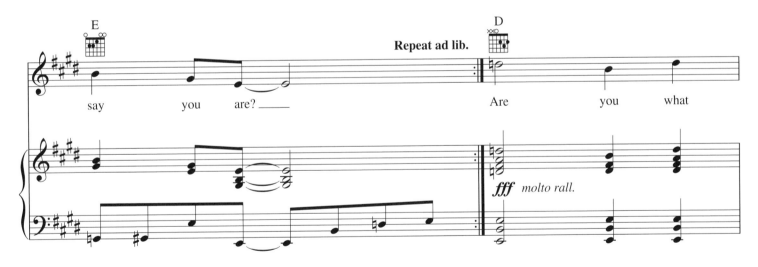

say you are? _____ Are you what

Repeat ad lib.

fff *molto rall.*

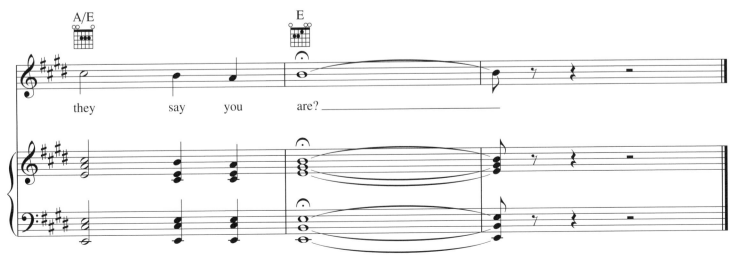

they say you are? _____

THERE IS A REASON

Words and Music by
RON BLOCK

Easy Country Ballad

I've seen hard times,

and I've been told there isn't an-y won-

-der that I fall.

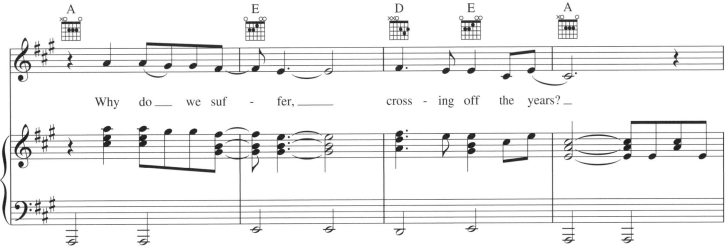

Why do — we suf - fer, _____ cross - ing off the years? _

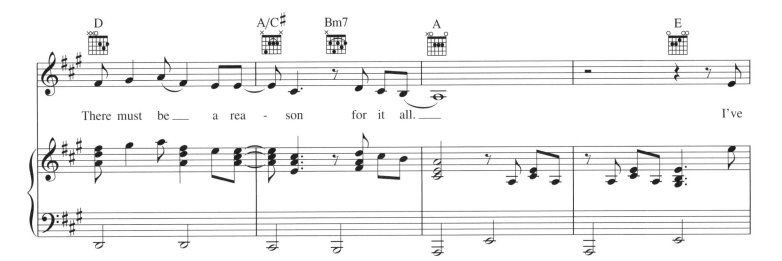

There must be __ a rea - son for it all. __ I've

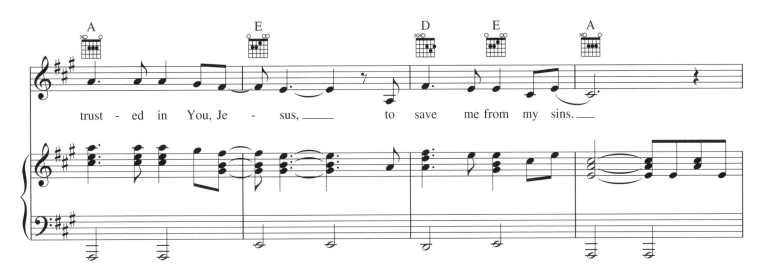

trust - ed in You, Je - sus, _____ to save me from my sins. __

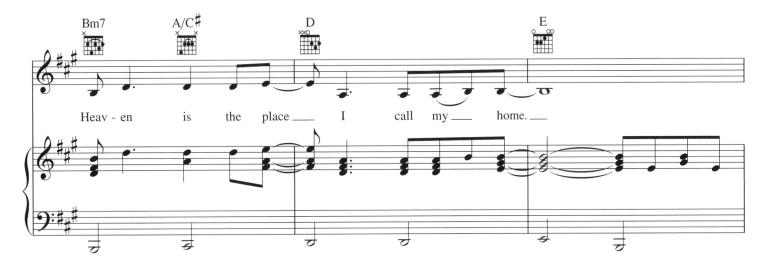

Heav - en is the place __ I call my __ home. __

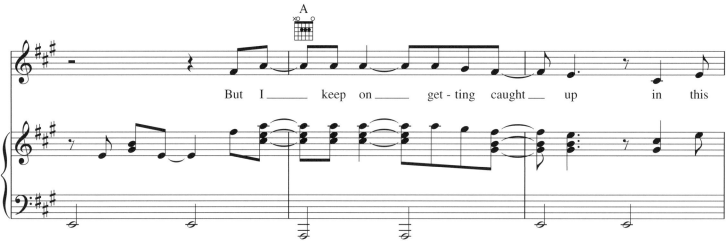

But I _____ keep on _____ get-ting caught _____ up in this

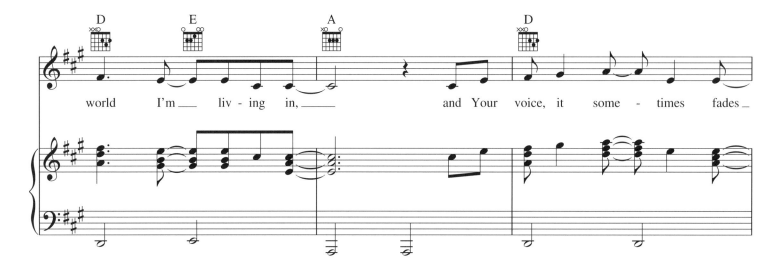

world I'm _____ liv-ing in, _____ and Your voice, it some-times fades _

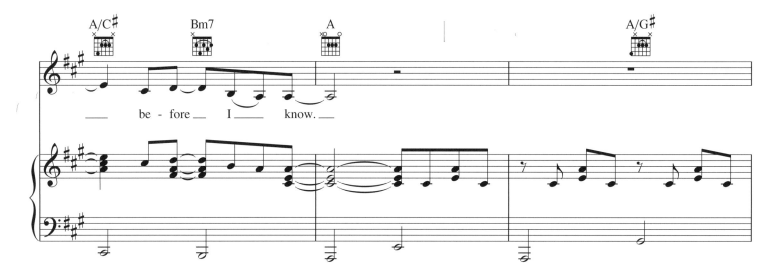

_____ be-fore _____ I _____ know. _____

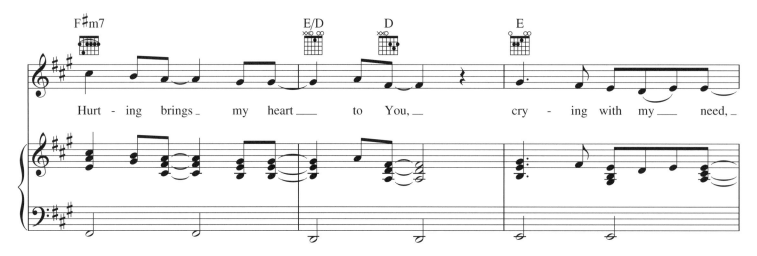

Hurt-ing brings _ my heart _____ to You, _ cry-ing with my _____ need, _

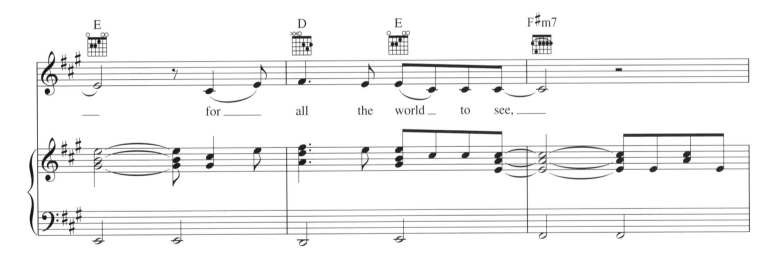

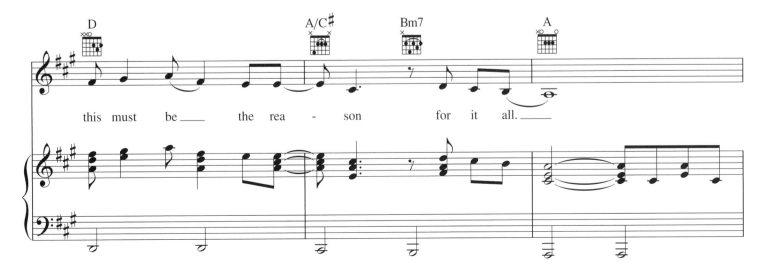

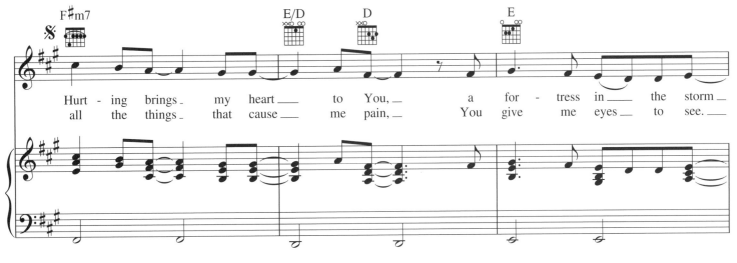

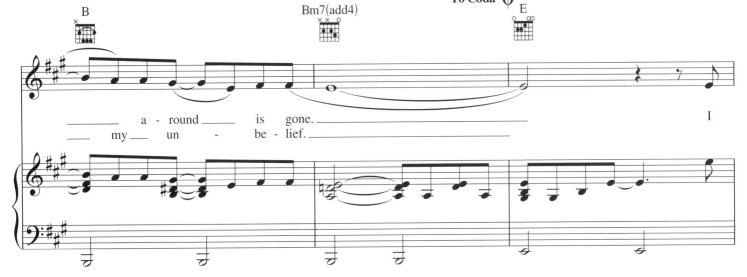

when the One who loves ___ me most ___ will give _____ me all. ___

D.S. al Coda

In

CODA

I've ___ seen hard ___ times, ___ and I've _____ been ___

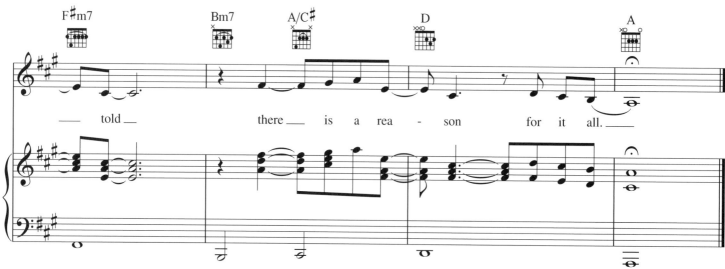

___ told ___ there ___ is a rea - son for it all. ___

WHEN I GET WHERE I'M GOIN'

Words and Music by RIVERS RUTHERFORD
and GEORGE TEREN

Moderately fast

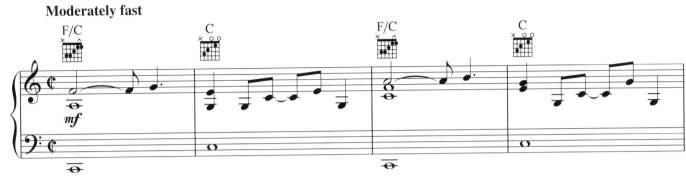

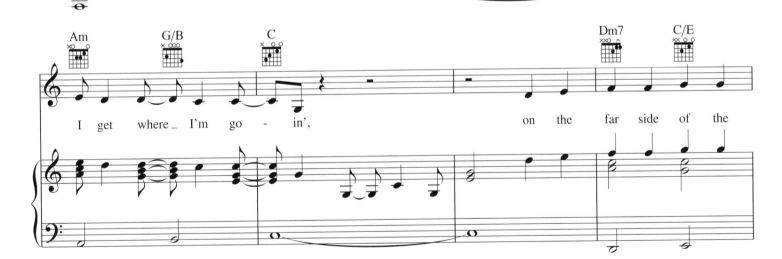

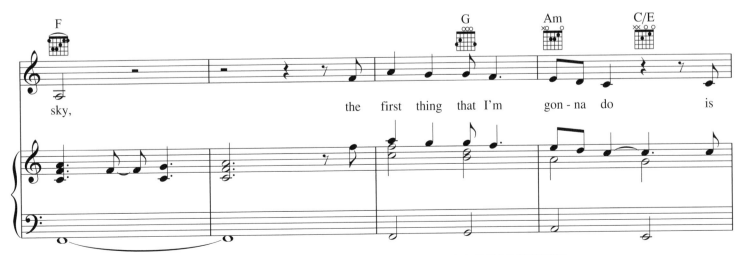

spread my wings and fly. I'm gon- na land be - side ___ a

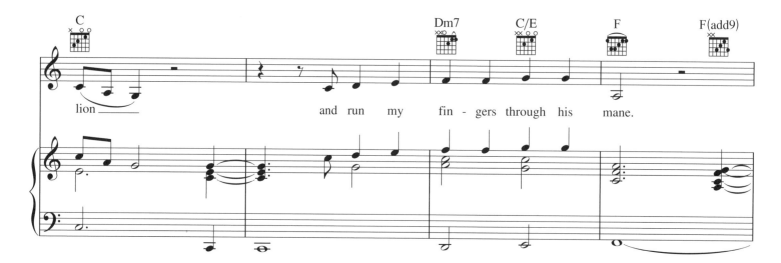

lion ___ and run my fin- gers through his mane.

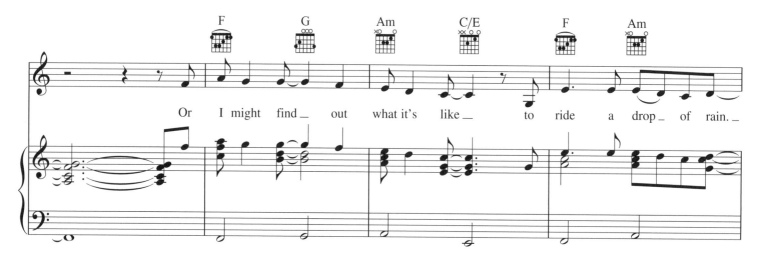

Or I might find ___ out what it's like ___ to ride a drop ___ of rain. ___

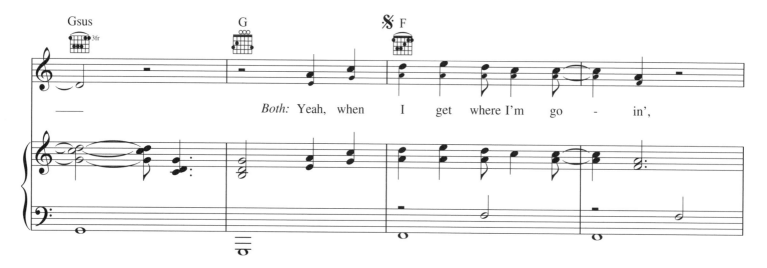

___ *Both:* Yeah, when I get where I'm go - in',

there'll be on - ly hap - py tears.____

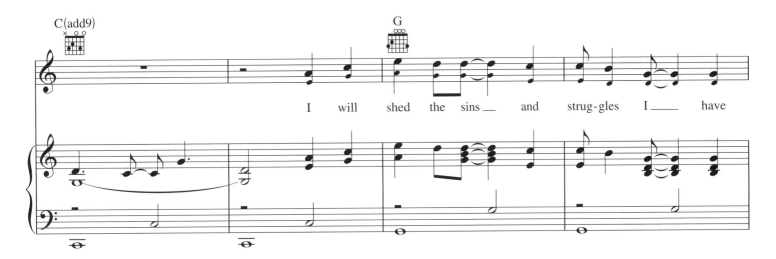

I will shed the sins____ and strug-gles I____ have

car - ried all____ these years.____ And I'll leave my heart wide o - pen,

I will love and have____ no fear.____

Yeah, when I get where I'm go - in', _____

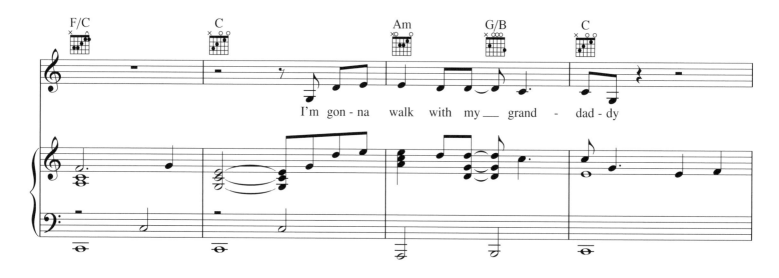

Male: don't cry for me _____ down here. _____

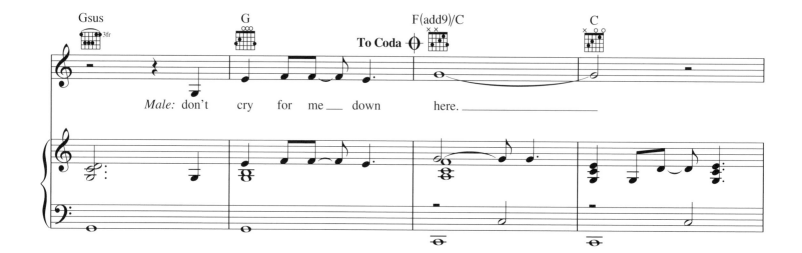

I'm gon - na walk with my _____ grand - dad - dy

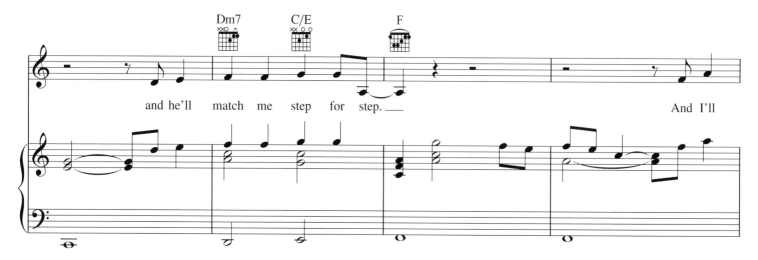

and he'll match me step for step. _____ And I'll

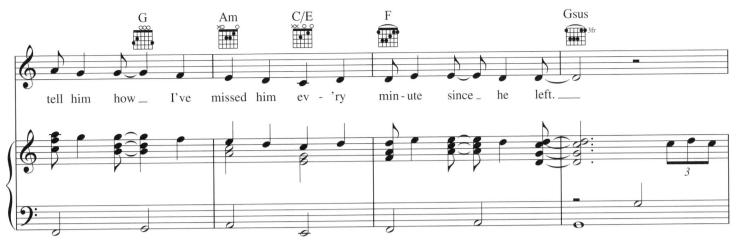

tell him how ___ I've missed him ev - 'ry min - ute since ___ he left. ___

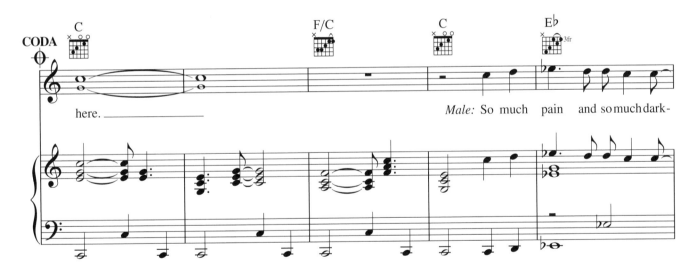

D.S. al Coda

And then I'll hug ___ his neck. *Both:* Yeah, when

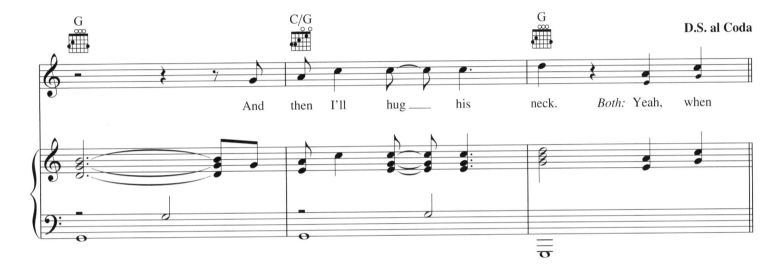

CODA

here. _____

Male: So much pain and so much dark-

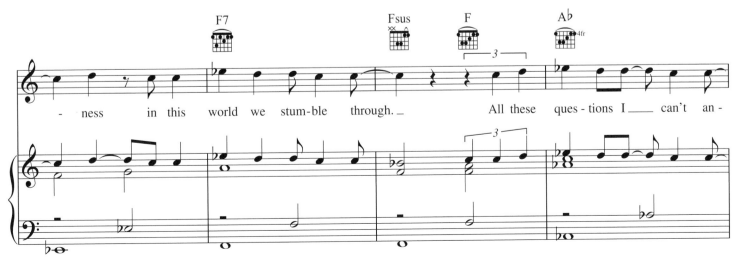

- ness in this world we stum - ble through. ___ All these ques - tions I ___ can't an -

-swer and so much work to do.

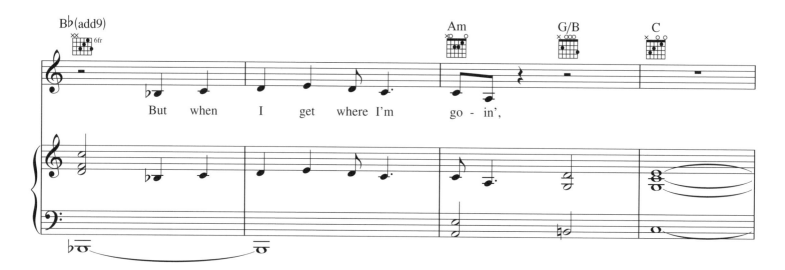

B♭(add9)

But when I get where I'm go - in',

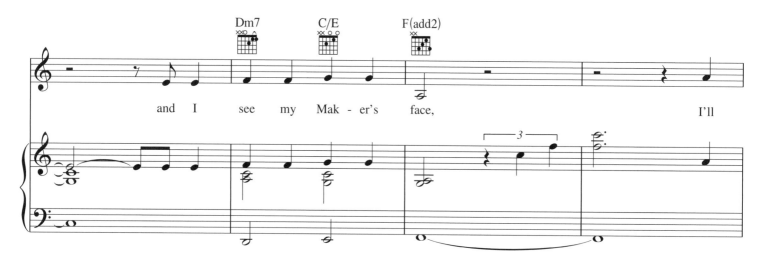

Dm7   C/E   F(add2)

and I see my Mak - er's face,   I'll

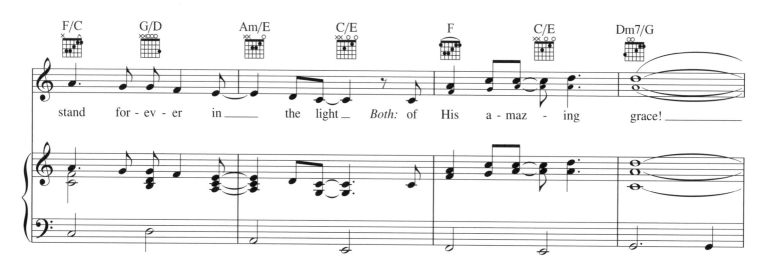

F/C   G/D   Am/E   C/E   F   C/E   Dm7/G

stand for - ev - er in ___ the light ___ *Both:* of His a - maz - ing grace! ___

Both: Yeah, when I _____ get where I'm

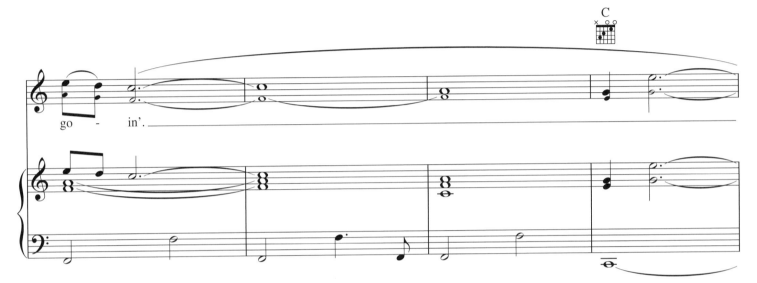

go - in'. _____

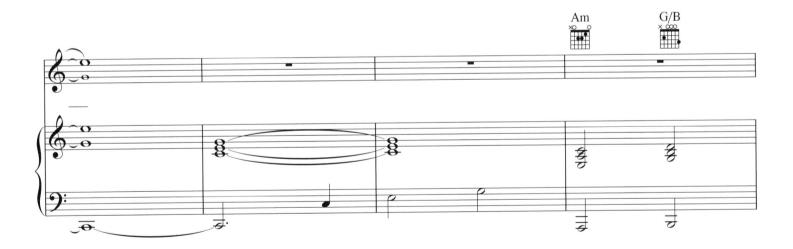

rit.

THREE WOODEN CROSSES

Words and Music by KIM WILLIAMS
and DOUG JOHNSON

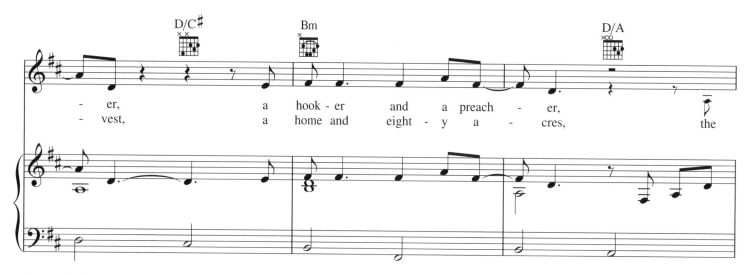

Recorded a half step lower.

rid - in' on ___ a mid - night bus, ___ bound for Mex - i - co.
faith and love ___ for grow - in' things ___ in his young son's ___

heart.
One was head - ed for ___ va - ca - tion, one for
And that teach - er left ___ her wis - dom in the

high - er ed - u - ca - tion and two of them ___ were search -
minds ___ of lots of chil - dren. Did her best to give ___ 'em all ___

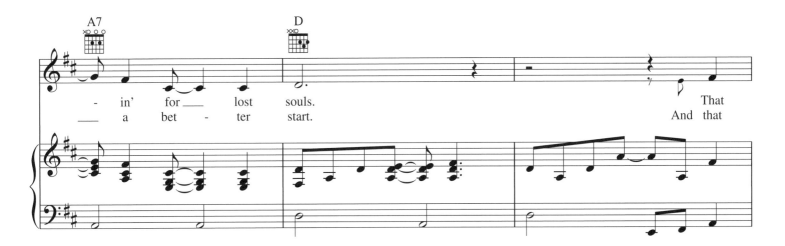

- in' for ___ lost souls.
___ a bet - ter start.
That
And that

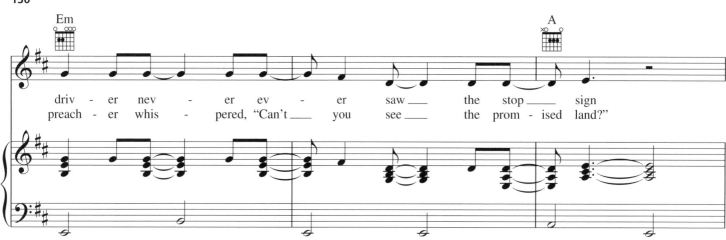

driv - er nev - er ev - er saw the stop sign
preach - er whis - pered, "Can't you see the prom - ised land?"

and eight - een - wheel - ers can't stop on a dime.
as he lay his blood-stained Bi - ble in that hook - er's hand.

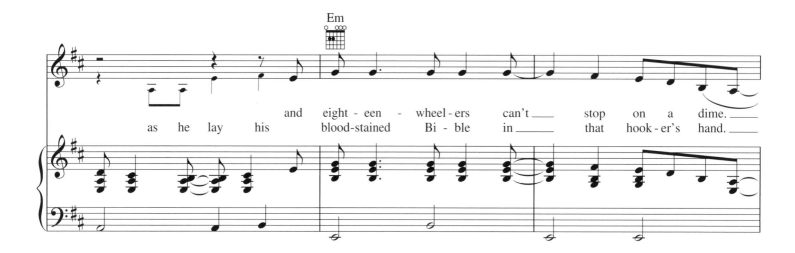

There are three wood - en cross -

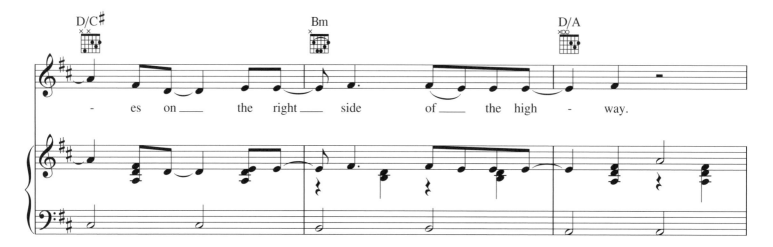

- es on the right side of the high - way.

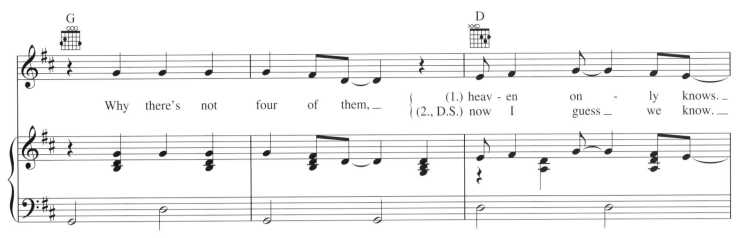

Why there's not four of them, __ { (1.) heav - en on - ly knows. __
{ (2., D.S.) now I guess __ we know. __

__ } I guess it's not what you take __ when you leave __

__ this world __ be - hind __ you, it's what you leave __ be - hind __

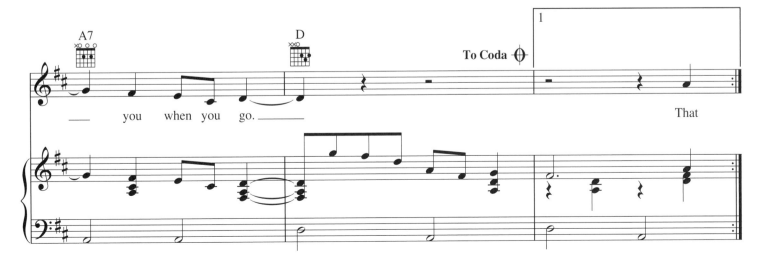

__ you when you go. __

That

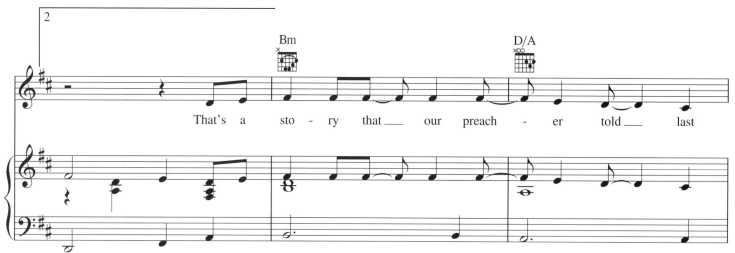

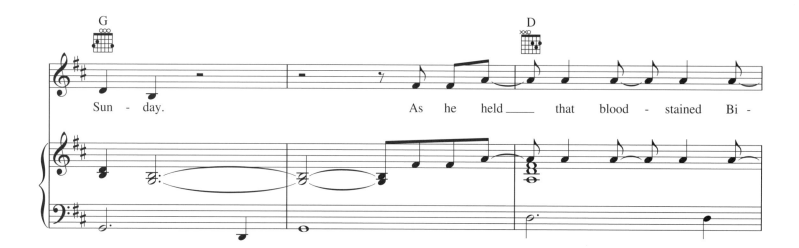

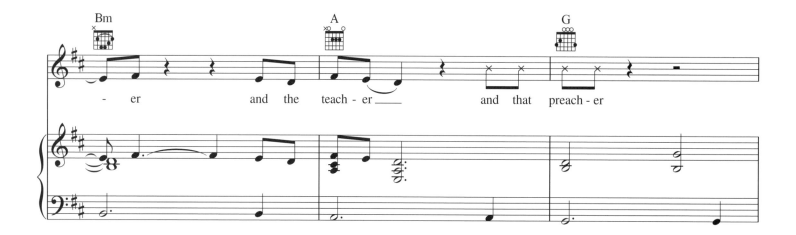

Em

who gave this Bi - ble to ___ my ma - ma who

A

read it ___ to me." _____

D.S. al Coda

There are

CODA

There are three wood - en cross -

D/C#   Bm   A   D

- es on ___ the right ___ side of _____ the high - way.

rit.

TURN! TURN! TURN!
(To Everything There Is a Season)

Words from the Book of Ecclesiastes
Adaptation and Music by PETE SEEGER

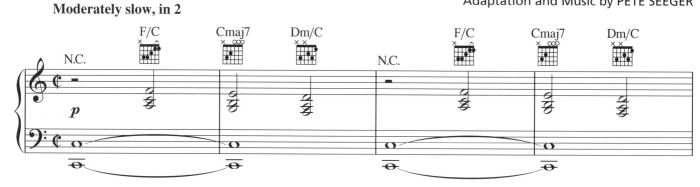

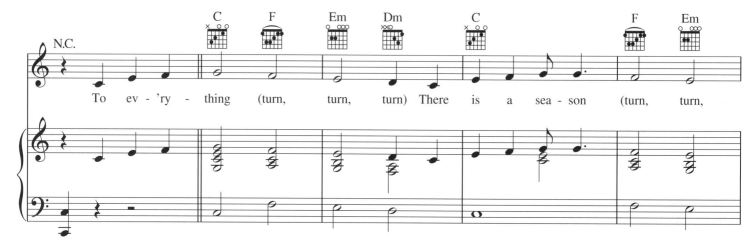

To ev-'ry-thing (turn, turn, turn) There is a sea-son (turn, turn,

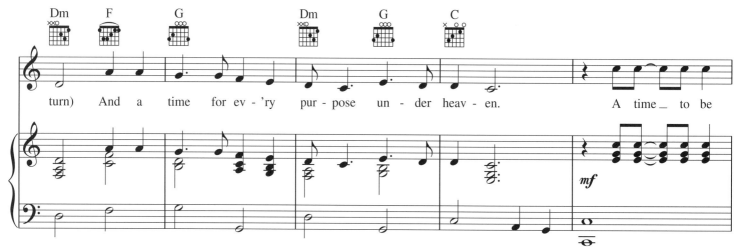

turn) And a time for ev-'ry pur-pose un-der heav-en. A time ___ to be

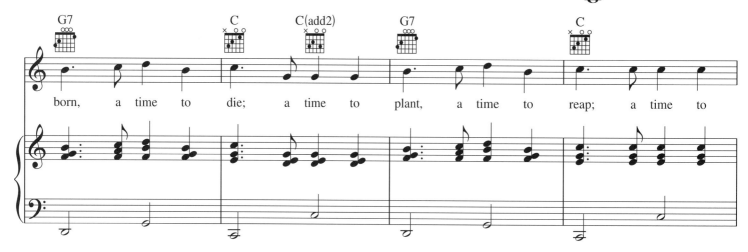

born, a time to die; a time to plant, a time to reap; a time to

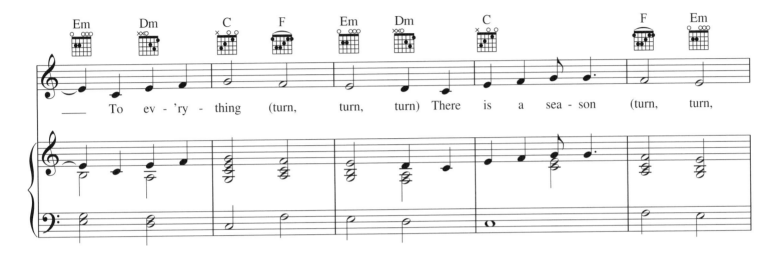

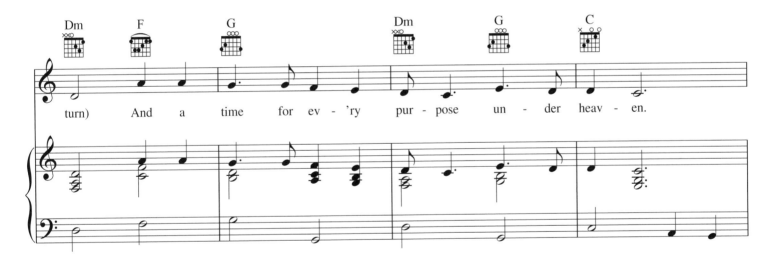

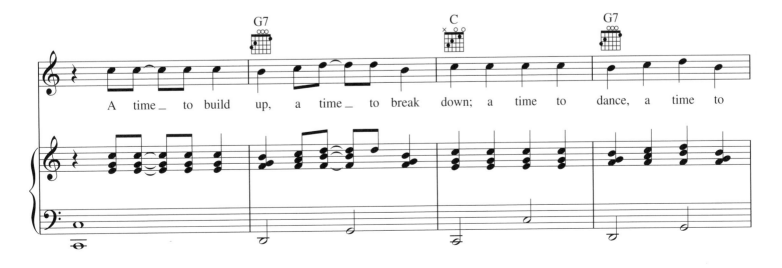

mourn; a time to cast __ a - way stones, a time to gath - er stones __

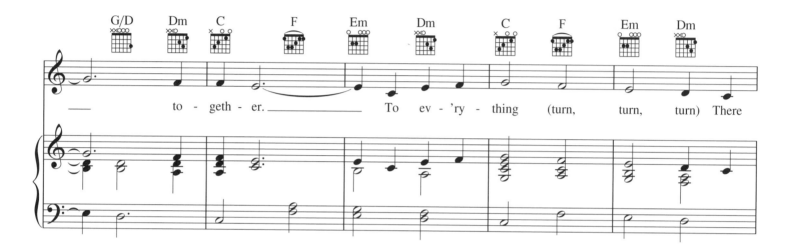

__ to - geth - er. _____ To ev - 'ry - thing (turn, turn, turn) There

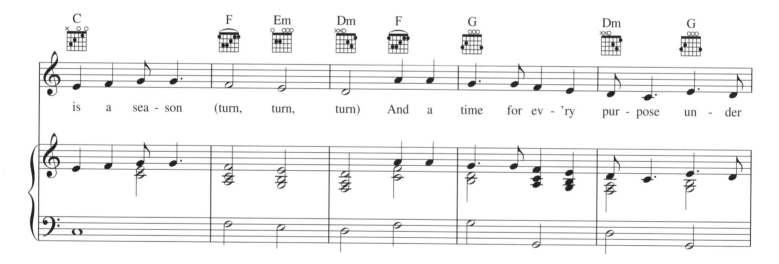

is a sea - son (turn, turn, turn) And a time for ev - 'ry pur - pose un - der

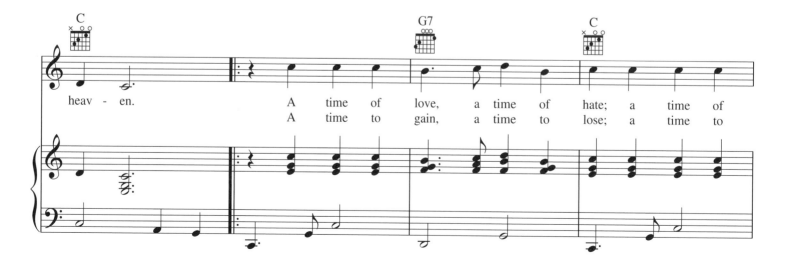

heav - en.

A time of love, a time of hate; a time of
A time to gain, a time to lose; a time to

YOU'LL NEVER WALK ALONE
from CAROUSEL

Lyrics by OSCAR HAMMERSTEIN II
Music by RICHARD RODGERS

Andantino molto cantabile

(with great warmth, like a hymn)

* alternate lyric: hold your head up high

blown _____ Walk on, walk on, with

hope in your heart, And you'll nev - er walk a -

lone, _____ You'll nev - er walk a -

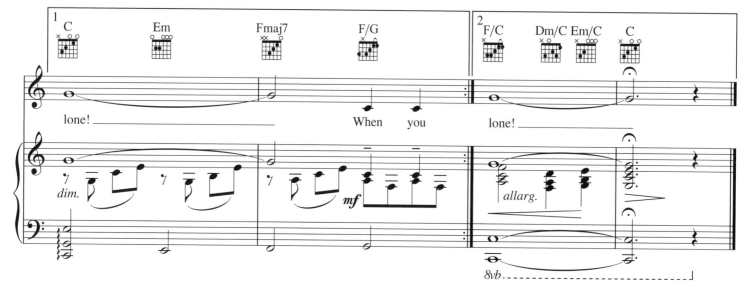

lone! When you lone! _____

WHY ME?
(Why Me, Lord?)

Words and Music by
KRIS KRISTOFFERSON

Moderately, with a Gospel feeling

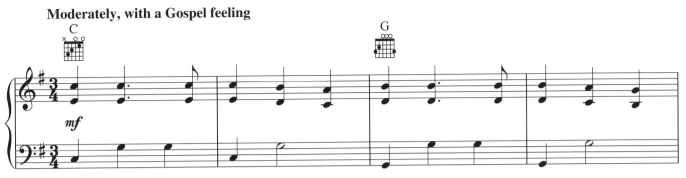

Why me, Lord?

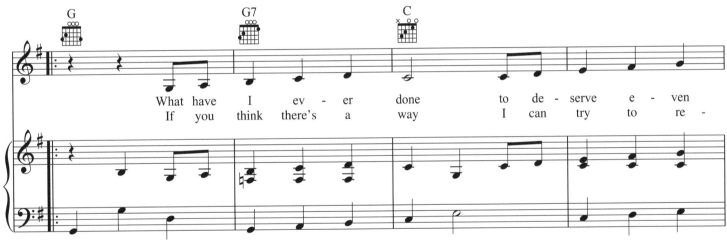

What have I ev-er done to de-serve e-ven

If you think there's a way I can try to re-

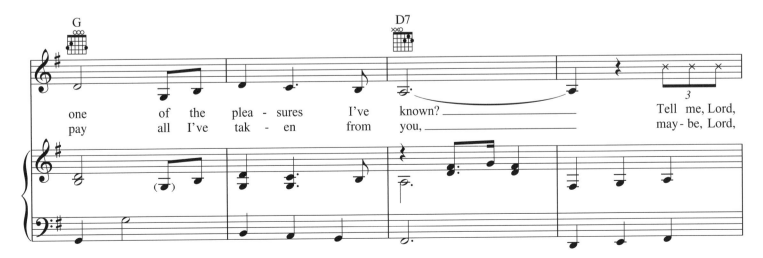

one of the plea-sures I've known?

pay all I've tak-en from you,

Tell me, Lord,

may-be, Lord,

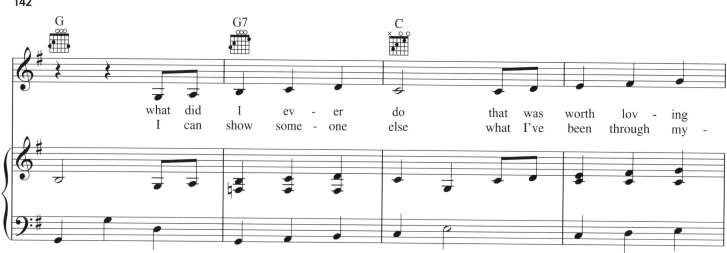

what did I ev - er do that was worth lov - ing
I can show some - one else what I've been through my -

you, or the kind - ness you've shown? _____
self, on my way back to you. _____

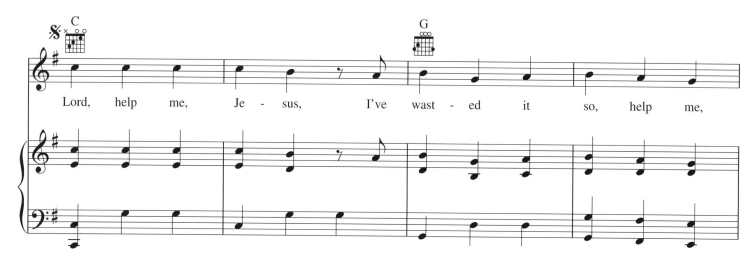

Lord, help me, Je - sus, I've wast - ed it so, help me,

Je - sus, I know what I am. _____ But

THE BEST EVER
COLLECTION
ARRANGED FOR PIANO, VOICE AND GUITAR

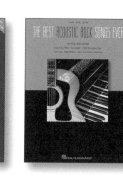

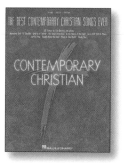

150 of the Most Beautiful Songs Ever
150 ballads
00360735 ....$24.95

150 More of the Most Beautiful Songs Ever
150 songs
00311318 ....$24.95

Best Acoustic Rock Songs Ever
65 acoustic hits
00310984 ....$19.95

Best Big Band Songs Ever
68 big band hits
00359129 ....$16.95

Best Broadway Songs Ever
83 songs
00309155 ....$24.95

More of the Best Broadway Songs Ever
82 songs
00311501 ....$22.95

Best Children's Songs Ever
102 tunes
00310360 (Easy Piano) $19.95

Best Christmas Songs Ever
69 holiday favorites
00359130 ....$19.95

Best Classic Rock Songs Ever
64 hits
00310800 ....$19.99

Best Classical Music Ever
86 classical favorites
00310674 (Piano Solo) $19.95

Best Contemporary Christian Songs Ever
50 favorites
00310558 ....$19.95

Best Country Songs Ever
78 classic country hits
00359135 ....$19.95

Best Early Rock 'n' Roll Songs Ever
74 songs
00310816 ....$19.95

Best Easy Listening Songs Ever
75 mellow favorites
00359193 ....$19.95

Best Gospel Songs Ever
80 gospel songs
00310503 ....$19.95

Best Hymns Ever
118 hymns
00310774 ....$18.95

Best Jazz Standards Ever
77 jazz hits
00311641 ....$19.95

More of the Best Jazz Standards Ever
74 beloved jazz hits
00311023 ....$19.95

Best Latin Songs Ever
67 songs
00310355 ....$19.95

Best Love Songs Ever
65 favorite love songs
00359198 ....$19.95

Best Movie Songs Ever
74 songs
00310063 ....$19.95

Best Praise & Worship Songs Ever
80 all-time favorites
00311057 ....$19.95

More of the Best Praise & Worship Songs Ever
80 songs
00311800 ....$19.99

Best R&B Songs Ever
66 songs
00310184 ....$19.95

Best Rock Songs Ever
63 songs
00490424 ....$18.95

Best Songs Ever
72 must-own classics
00359224 ....$22.95

More of the Best Songs Ever
79 more favorites
00310437 ....$19.95

Best Soul Songs Ever
70 hits
00311427 ....$19.95

Best Standards Ever, Vol. 1 (A-L)
72 beautiful ballads
00359231 ....$17.95

More of the Best Standards Ever, Vol. 1 (A-L)
76 all-time favorites
00310813 ....$17.95

Best Standards Ever, Vol. 2 (M-Z)
72 songs
00359232 ....$17.95

More of the Best Standards Ever, Vol. 2 (M-Z)
75 stunning standards
00310814 ....$17.95

Best Torch Songs Ever
70 sad and sultry favorites
00311027 ....$19.95

Best TV Songs Ever
64 catchy theme songs
00311048 ....$17.95

Best Wedding Songs Ever
70 songs
00311096 ....$19.95

FOR MORE INFORMATION, SEE YOUR LOCAL MUSIC DEALER, OR WRITE TO:

HAL•LEONARD®
CORPORATION
7777 W. BLUEMOUND RD. P.O. BOX 13819 MILWAUKEE, WI 53213

Visit us on-line for complete songlists at
www.halleonard.com

Prices, contents and availability subject to change without notice. Not all products available outside the U.S.A.

0309